hot cocoa
BOMBS

hot cocoa
BOMBS

DELICIOUS, FUN, AND CREATIVE HOT CHOCOLATE TREATS

NATALIE WISE

Skyhorse Publishing

Skyhorse Publishing books may be purchased in bulk at special discounts for sales promotion, corporate gifts, fund-raising, or educational purposes. Special editions can also be created to specifications. For details, contact the Special Sales Department, Skyhorse Publishing, 307 West 36th Street, 11th Floor, New York, NY 10018 or info@skyhorsepublishing.com.

Skyhorse® and Skyhorse Publishing® are registered trademarks of Skyhorse Publishing, Inc.®, a Delaware corporation.

Visit our website at www.skyhorsepublishing.com.

10 9 8 7 6 5 4 3 2

Library of Congress Cataloging-in-Publication Data
Names: Wise, Natalie, author.
Title: Hot cocoa bombs: delicious, fun, and creative hot chocolate treats!
  / Natalie Wise.
Description: New York: Skyhorse Publishing, [2021] | Summary: "50
  do-it-yourself hot chocolate bomb recipes for kids and adults"—
  Provided by publisher.
Identifiers: LCCN 2021022044 (print) | LCCN 2021022045 (ebook) | ISBN
  9781510767065 (hardcover) | ISBN 9781510768048 (epub)
Subjects: LCSH: Cooking (Chocolate) | Cooking (Cocoa) | Desserts. | LCGFT:
  Cookbooks.
Classification: LCC TX767.C5 W57 2021 (print) | LCC TX767.C5 (ebook) |
  DDC 641.6/374—dc23
LC record available at https://lccn.loc.gov/2021022044
LC ebook record available at https://lccn.loc.gov/2021022045

Cover design by Mumtaz Mustafa
Cover and interior images by Natalie Wise; photos on pages 114, 116, and 118 by Jessica Jean Weston

Print ISBN: 978-1-5107-6706-5
Ebook ISBN: 978-1-5107-6804-8

Printed in China

Table of Contents

Introduction

Hot cocoa bombs are all the rage, for good reason. Someone invented a new way to enjoy chocolate, which is cause for major celebration in my book. But can hot chocolate really be that new? Can it really be surprising and intriguing, imaginative and beguiling, magical and utterly delicious? Yes, yes it can. I'm here to help you create luscious, fantastical, beautiful, elegant, and chocolatey cocoa bombs your friends will clamor for, your children will delight in, and anyone lucky enough to receive one will think you are a master chocolatier (because you will be!).

Hot chocolate bombs, sometimes also called hot cocoa truffles or bonbons, are hollow chocolate spheres filled with dry hot cocoa mix. You place the whole cocoa bomb in a mug. When you pour hot milk (or another hot liquid) over the thin, hollow chocolate, the heat melts the chocolate "bomb" and anything inside the sphere "explodes" out of the chocolate shell into the liquid. Most bombs have hot cocoa mix, and then some combination of marshmallows, sprinkles, and all manner of other edible additions that you stir into the milk as well. Adding truffles or ganache as filling instead of a dry mix is another way to create different flavors and textures. Stir well, and you've got one extra-special cup of cocoa. Different, indeed.

Since round-shaped treats abound (cake pops, anyone?) and hollow chocolates (think chocolate Easter bunny!) filled with candy, cream, or treats are also popular around holidays, it's no surprise that someone may encounter a chocolate bomb and not realize what it is. A round, hollow chocolate . . . great. Oh, it makes a rattling noise when you pick it up! How fun. My friend made this mistake when she was gifted two beautifully-decorated hot cocoa bombs without instructions. She bit into the chocolate ball, and was unpleasantly surprised by a cloud of cocoa powder, which is a messy but understandable mistake. Luckily she was able to enjoy the second cocoa bomb the proper way!

Making a hollow chocolate sphere may seem difficult at first, but the process is quite simple once you've done it a few times and have a few tools at hand. A half-sphere mold is probably the only new thing you'll need to buy to get started. Of course, there are other options we'll discuss later, but silicone half-sphere molds are fantastic for beginners. Their flexibility allows you to easily pop the chocolate sphere halves out. Hot cocoa bombs are made in two pieces and "glued" together to create the full shape, either by melting the edges or by painting extra chocolate around the two halves and letting them set.

This two-half-sphere technique also allows you to add fillings, which might include sprinkles, edible glitter, golden edible pearls, or simply cocoa mix and marshmallows. Search the internet for sprinkles and you'll see an entire world has evolved from what used to be two choices: rainbow or chocolate. Now you'll find a dazzling array of metallic dragées, edible glitters, sugar shapes of all kinds and sprinkle mixes with names that sound like song titles or nail polish colors. There is also a whole new world of marshmallows to choose from. Regular mini marshmallows will work just fine and create a classic hot cocoa experience. But tiny dehydrated marshmallows like the ones that come in a standard package of hot cocoa mix are a fun addition, especially for mini bombs, and they allow more room for extras. Dehydrated mini marshmallows can be ordered online or found in the candy-making section of a craft store. There are also flavored, filled, and shaped marshmallows galore! Be sure to plan ahead as you'll probably want to special-order a few items for really unique fillings.

Once the two halves of the sphere are filled and attached, it's time to decorate! This might be the most exciting part. A packet of hot cocoa mix can probably be found in every home. However, a large, shiny, stunning globe of chocolate elevates humble cocoa mix to coveted-gift status. Much like cake pops, the exterior of chocolate bombs can be transformed into an endless number of circle-shaped themes: colored, painted, coated, drizzled, glittered, and bedazzled.

I've taken inspiration from everywhere to create a collection of unusual, unique, and surprising hot cocoa bombs. Not only have I included some of my local foodie friends and their expertise, I've traveled the world (flavor-wise) to create flavor combinations that would hopefully make Zumbo (one of Australia's top pastry/chocolate/sugar-chefs, known for his mind-bending creations) proud. From pop culture to Paris, from Mexico's hot chiles to Spain's churros, and from sugar-sweet-magical-unicorns to a divine chocolate-lover's bomb, I'm sure you'll find a new favorite or a few here. I've also included plenty of inspiration for you to create your *own* unique hot cocoa bombs. The ideas are absolutely endless, and I can't wait to see what you create, so don't forget to share (@bynataliewise on Instagram and #nataliewise on all social media platforms)!

Lastly, one little question: Is it a hot chocolate bomb or a hot cocoa bomb? The terms here are interchangeable, since the bomb is *made* out of chocolate, and has hot cocoa powder/mix *inside* it. Generally the distinction is negligible and likely to be related to what region you live in or what you grew up saying. However, there is a culinary distinction in that hot cocoa is made with cocoa powder and generally comes in a dry form that is mixed with hot milk or water. Hot chocolate, however, is more of a "drinking chocolate" that is made from pure chocolate melted into the milk or water. So whichever you prefer, carry on, because chocolate and cocoa are a match made in heaven. Let's make some!

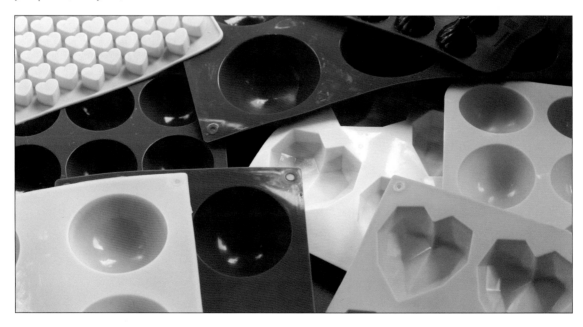

Getting Started

TOOLS

While making cocoa bombs is quite simple, the technique might seem a bit daunting at first, especially if you've never used chocolate molds. Don't worry! There are essentially two ways to make cocoa bombs: the simple way, with silicone molds and candy melts, or the expert way, with polycarbonate molds and tempered chocolate. Of course, you can use candy melts in polycarbonate molds and tempered chocolate in silicone molds. I just want to assure you, you can do this. You don't need to invest in expensive polycarbonate molds or have already mastered chocolatiering techniques to make beautiful cocoa bombs. Start simple, and learn as you go. Here are some of the basic tools you might want.

Molds

The two main choices for half-sphere chocolate molds are silicone or polycarbonate. The biggest difference is that silicone is 100 percent flexible and polycarbonate has zero flexibility. Polycarbonate has been the choice of professional chocolate makers for decades as the sturdiness creates a perfect shape over and over and the molds last for years. There's no need to put them on baking sheets or risk spilling the entire mold. Polycarbonate molds are less forgiving, though; if your chocolate is not properly tempered it will not come out of the mold. Candy melts are one way around this problem, as they don't need to be tempered and will come out of polycarbonate molds. It is much easier to create a perfect sphere with straight edges that line up beautifully when using a polycarbonate mold. On the other hand, silicone is perfect for beginners due to its flexibility that allows even imperfect chocolate half spheres to be unmolded. They do need to be stabilized on cookie sheets, as once they are full of chocolate they can be tricky things to maneuver from counter to refrigerator.

There is a price difference as well; silicone molds are much less expensive than polycarbonate. Polycarbonate molds are professional quality and made to last for decades, which is reflected in the price. Start with silicone to see how much you enjoy making these, or go straight for professional molds with full confidence. There is no wrong choice, and both will make beautiful bombs.

The standard size used in this book is a 2.5-inch-diameter mold as well as a smaller 2-inch-diameter mold. Other size/shape molds are used occasionally. A larger 3-inch mold can be enticing, because it offers more room for fillings and looks rather impressive. However, the problem is actually practical: most mugs have a 3-inch diameter and the cocoa bomb will not fit inside them! Keep this in mind.

Any 3-D shape that isn't too intricate and has two halves that are easily matched should work in theory, so feel free to experiment. If the 3-D shape is too deep, or doesn't make sense with two similar halves, try using the technique applied to the gingerbread men on page 81. Simply filling the mold halfway with chocolate and pressing the cocoa mix and marshmallows into the back of it might be an option, so take a look at those instructions.

If you don't want to purchase any molds right away, no worries! You can use smooth-interior apple-sauce, fruit or pudding containers, yogurt cups, egg-shaped candy containers, or small paper cups. Get creative . . . the worst that could happen is it won't look pretty, but it will still be chocolate!

Never put any kind of chocolate mold in the dishwasher, even if they say they're dishwasher-safe. The high heat may cause warping, powdered dishwasher detergents are abrasive, and hard-water buildup can leave your molds (and cocoa bombs!) cloudy. Make sure to hand-wash both silicone and polycarbonate molds with a soft, non-scratch sponge, as a rough sponge could put small scratches on the surface. You might not notice them at first, but slowly your chocolate will become less and less glossy as it finds its way into the minute scratches.

One other note: It's best to reserve some molds for milk and dark chocolate, and some for white. You might also wish to have a set for colored chocolate. Label them with a permanent marker (silicone) or masking tape (polycarbonate). No matter how well you wash them, it seems stray bits of dark chocolate will find their way onto your beautiful white chocolate shells. Keeping the two separate is best for beautiful bombs.

Thermometer

If you plan to try tempering chocolate at all, you'll want a thermometer. A good old-fashioned candy or deep frying thermometer will work, as will a probe thermometer (usually for meat), or any kitchen thermometer. Don't go to your medicine cabinet though; keep this one strictly for kitchen use! There are a few other types of thermometers that work especially well for tempering chocolate, too. Candy melts do not require a thermometer, so if you're simply using candy melts you won't need to add a thermometer to your list.

Candy Thermometer: These are usually a thick glass tube with a clip to attach to the side of the pan as you watch sugar mixtures boil during candymaking. If you don't have one, certainly your mom, grandma, or neighbor has one. This type of thermometer will work; you'll just need to make sure you work in a batch of chocolate large enough for the thermometer to accurately catch even small adjustments in temperature— at least one pound of chocolate. Since most of these are a liquid-in-glass style, it is harder to be totally accurate, which is of the utmost importance in chocolate tempering.

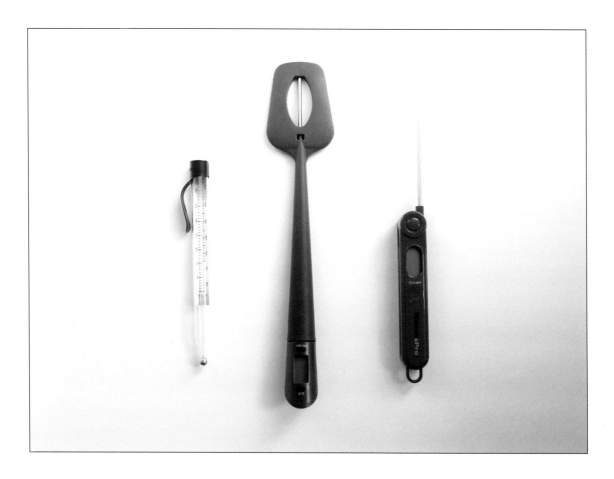

Meat/Probe Thermometer: If you grill a lot, I bet you have one of these handy gadgets in your kitchen, usually with a large round dial or a digital display. This will be much easier to work with because the probe is thinner, allowing you to temper a smaller batch of chocolate, and if it is digital, you'll get much more accurate readings. However, the probe can be very short, designed only to go into the depth of a steak, so look for one with a longer, grill-style probe that won't touch the mixture or cause your hand to be too close to hot mixtures.

Infrared Digital Thermometer: These touchless wonders are well-known in the medical world, but they also make them for the food industry. Press a button and point it at something and a tiny bit of thermal radiation is emitted to instantly take a temperature. This certainly cuts down on the mess, but it can be less accurate and also requires you to stop stirring entirely to take a temperature reading, which may result in scorching.

Candy-Making Spatula Thermometer: Candy-making spatula thermometers are just what they sound like: spatulas designed for candy-making that have an internal thermometer. The best part is, you can pull the handle out to convert this into a probe thermometer for smaller jobs. These are my favorite because they give you options, and let you take the temperature as you're moving the chocolate.

Double-Boilers, Spatulas, Bowls, and More

The right tools can make the difference between bakery-quality hot cocoa bombs and Pinterest-fail hot cocoa bombs.

A double-boiler is perfect for tempering chocolate without worrying about getting it too hot or scorching in the microwave. A double-boiler probably sounds like something grandma used and you scratch your head to think if you might have one in that above-the-refrigerator cabinet. A double-boiler is a two-piece set that usually looks like two pans, but one will have a rounded bottom, and it sits inside the second pan. Doubler boilers are made to heat things gently, that is, you aren't actually boiling the liquid in the top piece, but only heating it by boiling the water in the pan below. This is exactly what you'll need for tempering chocolate. But it doesn't actually need to be a true double-boiler. Trust me, I understand not wanting to add another large gadget to your cabinets. You can easily create one by using a metal or heat-proof glass bowl that fits inside a pot that holds at least 2 inches of water that the bowl doesn't touch. Test this by filling the pot with 2 inches of water and setting the empty bowl on top. Remove the bowl. Is the bottom wet? If so, try a different pot and bowl combination. If not, voila, you've got yourself a double-boiler!

If you're just using candy melts, or are using a microwave method of tempering your chocolate, you'll need a plastic, microwave-safe bowl. You might not think the bowl you're using matters, but I've made hundreds and hundreds of cocoa bombs, so trust me: it does. Not all plastic bowls are microwave-safe, so be *sure* to use one labeled as such. The reason? Glass and ceramic bowls are great at holding heat, but you do not want that when melting chocolate or candy melts, because overheating it ruins the entire batch. The residual heat from a glass or ceramic bowl can cause that overheating.

I recommend silicone spatulas for stirring and melting your chocolate, as they allow you to thoroughly mix all the chocolate from the bottom and sides to prevent scorching. A spoon or other metal

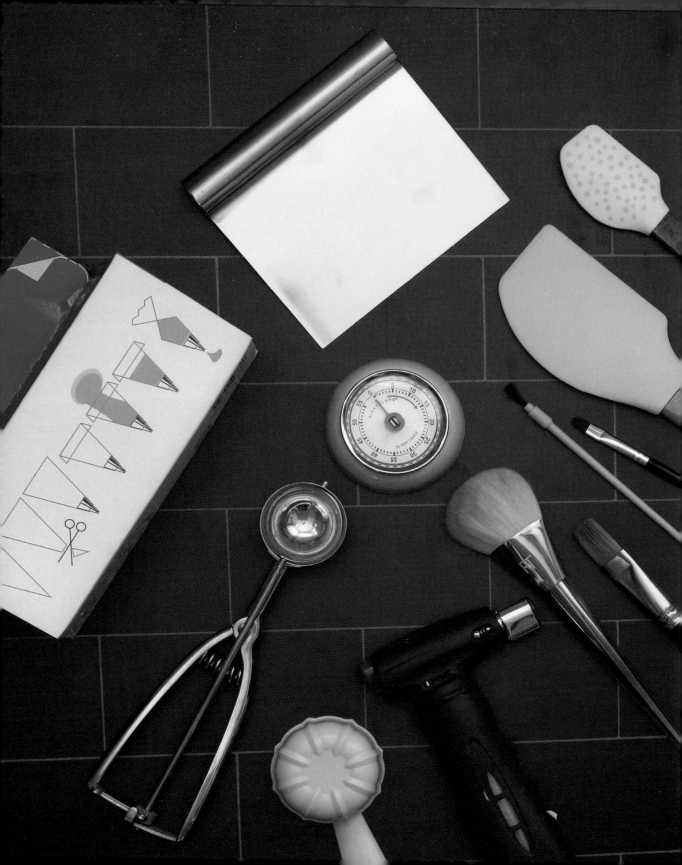

implement is likely to miss parts of the chocolate, resulting in uneven melting. Don't use a whisk for the chocolate as it will incorporate too much air.

To make sure each cocoa bomb shell contains the same amount of chocolate and thereby ensuring they taste exactly the same each time, I like to use a cupcake batter scoop for filling the molds. This is the kind with a spring-loaded handle that easily drops the entire amount of batter or filling into the mold. The small-size scoop I use holds approximately one tablespoon. Using the scoop is also much less messy than pouring or spooning, which results in lots of stray chocolate that, when you're releasing the spheres, can break the edges they are attached to. This also makes sure you have enough chocolate to fill all the molds and won't end up with an odd number of shells because one was overfilled.

If you're using polycarbonate molds, you'll also want a metal scraper or bench scraper to smooth the edges perfectly and clean the mold edges. Metal works best here for a perfectly sharp edge. Don't worry, if you use it on an angle you won't scrape your molds. If you don't have a pastry bench scraper, you might have a metal scraper used to corral chopped veggies.

You'll need a wide, shallow pan to heat on the stove to melt the edges of your cocoa bombs to stick them together. You can also use a ¼ sheet pan placed over the burner for more working room, but be *sure* to be very careful as the sheet pan will be hot all around and obviously does not have a handle. You only need very, very low heat to melt the chocolate shells, so don't overheat your pan or the chocolate that is already melted will burn. You can also try microwaving an empty plate (be sure to wear oven mitts when removing it from the microwave and set it on a heat-proof surface) and using that as the hot surface to melt the edges. The microwaved-plate method is much safer if you have teens or kids helping, but still be very careful with this part! If you prefer not to have heat involved at all, you can use melted chocolate and your small brush to brush the warm chocolate on each edge and push them together. This may result in a slightly messier look, but that is easily solved by rolling the edges in sprinkles.

When decorating, I like to use a silicone mat to hold my shells stable while I work. This is much less slippery than waxed or parchment paper, won't leave an indent like a cooling rack might, and is not too deep like a muffin tin would be. The texture is perfect for gripping the shells slightly, keeping all extra sprinkles and powders contained, and easily lifting off with no damage to the chocolate. However, if you don't have one, I recommend turning your silicone molds upside down and placing the shells between the cups, raised on top of them. You'll be able to achieve a similar result.

Piping bags or small zipper food-storage bags will be very helpful in decorating. I like to use 12-inch piping bags, as they are sturdier than food-storage bags and therefore produce a straighter line, but you might not have these handy. Most decorating in this book doesn't require any piping tips; simply snip a corner of whichever bag you're using.

A timer is great to have to remind you that your shells are in the refrigerator or freezer! Leaving them in there too long can cause condensation damage.

If you find fingerprints all over your chocolates, you might want to grab a pair of cotton chocolate-work gloves. These are specifically made for handling dry, finished chocolates without adding fingerprints.

If you find your molds have a cloudy build-up, it's likely from the cocoa butter or oil in the chocolate or candy melts. A small spray bottle with undiluted vodka in it (yes, I know! vodka!) and a small cotton pad or cloth can be used to remove this and is food-safe, so do it right before you use the molds, letting it air-dry, for perfectly shiny chocolate.

INGREDIENTS

Food Coloring

Food coloring is tricky when it comes to chocolate treats and beverages, as there are different uses for different kinds of food colorings. Everyone probably has a little box set of the primary colors of liquid food coloring; a few of you might be able to scrounge up some gel colors if you dig in the baking drawer. The problem with both of those types of food colorings is that they contain water, and water and chocolate do not mix. Nor do water and dry mixes inside the cocoa bombs! You may want to invest in a few other types of food coloring if you decide you really enjoy making cocoa bombs. Most of these can be found in the cake- and candy-making aisle of your local crafts store.

Powdered Food Coloring: Powdered food colors will be used to color the beverages. They are added to the dry cocoa mixes that go inside the cocoa bomb shells and create color once mixed with the hot milk. Of course, if you added a liquid food coloring inside the cocoa bomb, it would become a small glob with the dry ingredients and be nearly impossible to whisk into the finished drink (though it's possible, if all else fails). Look for natural powder food colorings. They may have slightly less vibrant colors when powdered, but are just as vibrant when added to liquids, and are made from fruits and vegetables

(and flowers, oddly enough . . . my favorite green powder is made from gardenias!). Make sure the powder food coloring you're purchasing for the interior mixes is water-soluble; some are made to go into oil-based mixtures and might color your drink but will also leave undissolved powder that you would have to strain out. Most powdered food colorings can also be used to color your chocolate, so these are great for a starter kit for making cocoa bombs.

Petal Dust: Petal dust is, in my opinion, like powdered pastel chalk—not literally, but figuratively. It's intensely pigmented, which means it will and does stain anything it comes in contact with, at least temporarily, so use this with great caution. It's generally used by cake makers to color, well, flowers, realistically, hence the name petal dust. Petal dust is only for finishing touches, not for adding to the drink mixes or coloring the chocolate.

Oil-Based: Oil-based food colorings are just like what they sound—food colorings that are oil-based. They come in small bottles in any number of shades, can be gradually added or mixed, and can create nearly any color you can imagine. They are specifically formulated without water and are what is used to color chocolate. White chocolate, mostly. Since they are oil-based, they may stain clothing, wood cutting boards, or counter surfaces, etc. if not cleaned immediately, so use with caution. I love oil-based food colorings because they are buildable—one drop creates a slight tint and ten creates a beautiful saturated color. You may need to search online for oil-based food colorings or go to a larger store stocked with more specialty cake- and candy-making supplies. The most common brands are ChefMaster and Colour Mill from Australia, and they both make a fantastic range of shades. Wilton also makes what they call "candy colors" for candy melts, but in a limited range of shades.

Flavor Oils

Adding flavor to chocolate requires oil-based flavorings instead of your standard baking extracts. Unfortunately, standard extracts contain water that will seize and ruin your chocolate, much like regular food colorings. There are many natural flavor oils, but your flavor profiles will be limited. The blend of natural and artificial flavorings will open up a wide range of flavors that are impossible to incorporate into chocolate or dry mixes otherwise, which is why I use them in this book. I use natural flavor oils whenever I can, but you'll need to be sure they are *not* water-soluble. The type of oils you'll be adding to chocolate are usually called candymaking flavors or flavor oils, as they are used to flavor all types of candies, but that label alone does not necessarily mean they are suitable for chocolate, so be sure to read their description carefully. Keep in mind you can make any of these recipes without adding the flavor oils to the chocolate; they are always optional. But when you start gathering candymaking flavors, it can get addictive; as you can see, I have a large collection!

Candymaking Flavors/Oils: LorAnn creates one of the most easily-available flavor oils for candymaking, both natural and artificial. A small portion of their wide range can usually be found in the cake- and candy-making aisle of your large grocery store or craft store. These flavor oils usually come in tiny 1-ounce bottles or larger 3-ounce bottles. I also love the flavors from One on One Flavoring and from Nature's Flavors. Look only for oil- or PG-based flavors (PG is propylene glycol). You can also search online "flavoring for chocolate" with whichever flavor you're trying to recreate, and chances are you'll find a version! You can leave the flavor oils out completely, but, of course, that will mean your flavor profile changes, becomes much less prominent, or disappears altogether. Since we're talking literally drops of flavor oils, I highly recommend you try them and see the difference they make in flavoring your cocoa bombs.

Food-Grade Essential Oils: Some of the natural food oils you might come across are actually food-grade essential oils. These are plant-based flavors by nature, such as clove, anise, cardamom, lemon, mint, etc. These are absolutely *not* your run-of-the-mill essential oils that you might use for cleaning or scent in a diffuser. These are strictly quality-controlled, tested, and labeled as food-safe. So make sure you research carefully and order new food-grade essential oils to use in your cocoa bomb-making instead of grabbing the ones under your kitchen sink or in your bathroom. Of course, food-grade essential oils must still be used in a safe manner and in small doses. Please do your own research and only use these food-grade essential oils if you feel comfortable and confident in doing so.

Chocolate

Chocolate. The basis of a hot cocoa bomb. It sounds so simple, yet gets complicated so quickly! There are a few main categories of chocolate that you might want to use for cocoa bomb making, so I'll try to simplify by sticking to those. But first, it needs to be said to never use regular baking chocolate chips for cocoa bombs. You will be sad. This type of chocolate is designed to hold its shape while being baked, so it will not melt properly, and will not come out of polycarbonate molds. It will never be shiny and it will never properly harden, even if you attempt to temper it, so if all you have is chocolate chips, *wait* to try making these until you can scrounge together some bar chocolate from various snack drawers in your house or you can get to the store. I know that sounds harsh, but I want you to be happy with your results! Below are the three main types of chocolate that will create beautiful results that will make everyone "ooo!" and "ahh!" over your creations. We'll get to how and why you might need to temper your chocolate in the next section.

Chocolate with Cocoa Butter: This is "real" chocolate, meltable to different liquidity depending on the percentage of cocoa butter in it. This type of chocolate is nearly always sold in bar form, either thin bars for eating or thick, hefty chunks for baking. This chocolate will need to be tempered to be used for cocoa bombs.

Couverture Chocolate: Also "real" chocolate, couverture is a specific type of chocolate created to be melted and tempered. Couverture is what candymakers tend to use. This type of chocolate usually comes in round tablets or wafers, and you will likely need to special order them. These also need to be tempered, even though they may look like the candymaking wafers. Don't be fooled and read your package carefully. You'll find milk and dark chocolates, as well as "white chocolate," though white chocolate does not have cocoa solids so it is not technically chocolate. Ghirardelli and Merckens couverture chocolates are my favorite.

Candymaking Wafers/Candy Coating Chocolate/Compound Chocolate/Dipping Chocolate/Almond Bark: This "chocolate" (it is not considered "real" chocolate as it does not contain cocoa butter) goes by many different names. It usually comes in block form or flat, round wafers, and is specifically designed for candy makers who do not want to temper chocolate but want a professional finish. It works perfectly for cocoa bombs and will create a shiny, hard shell nearly every time. Candy coatings come in many colors, so you won't need to seek out oil-based food coloring. Chocolate and white chocolate candy-making coatings are readily available at almost all grocery stores, making it perfect for beginners. The downside is, as this is not true chocolate, it is not high-quality chocolate, especially the colored wafers. The taste will suffer, but the ease of use and convenience might outweigh that. It is often overly sweet, which may affect your flavor combinations, or can have a waxy or unpleasant aftertaste. Ghirardelli and Merckens also make candymaking wafers that do not need to be tempered and taste quite good.

For ease of use, the term "chocolate" will be used interchangeably even with candy melts, as they have the same uses here and will be creating the same product. For instance, water should not mix with chocolate *or* candy melts, but I will simply say, "Chocolate and water do not mix!"

Fillings

Frosting, Truffles, Ganache: Frosting makes a wonderful addition to cocoa bombs! Not only is it perfectly sweet, store-bought or shelf-stable homemade frosting has such a creamy texture that melts perfectly into cocoa. It's also a fun variation on dry mixes and can add color and different flavors. I like to use a medium-size cookie batter scoop, usually around 2 tablespoons, that easily releases the perfect amount of frosting into each bomb. Hot cocoa bombs with frosting are best eaten within one week.

Homemade or store-bought truffles and ganache are another decadent filling for hot cocoa bombs. They're also an easy way to get flavors that might be difficult to recreate with only dry ingredients, such as champagne truffles in the Pink Champagne hot cocoa bomb, or key lime truffles in a Key Lime hot cocoa bomb.

Ganache is a mixture of chocolate and cream that stabilizes as it cools and remains shelf-stable (you don't need to refrigerate it) for a week or two if properly made. I've seen jars of ganache in the baking and ice cream topping sections as well. Make sure your ganache can be shelf-stable by reading the directions of your recipe or the jar. Since it does contain cream, you wouldn't want it to spoil if not kept refrigerated. The best part about ganache-filled cocoa bombs is that the ganache is already smooth and contains enough chocolate that you don't need to add a powdered mix and you'll get an intensely luxurious result that a dry mix can't compete with.

Truffles instantly elevate a hot cocoa bomb and seem rather fancy. They can be made at home easily but can seem intimidating, so feel free to purchase them. You can find truffles in just about every shape and flavor as well, and they are a great way to add adult flavors, such as rum or champagne. They also create a nice luxurious texture and can be used alone or along with a hot cocoa powder.

Hot Cocoa Powder and Other Powder Mixes

Of course, we are making hot cocoa bombs, so we'll need a hot cocoa mix for most of our creations! You can use any hot cocoa mix you'd like, from the standard grocery-store single-serve package to a luxury hot cocoa from your local chocolate shop.

Standard Hot Cocoa Mix: Don't be afraid to use your favorite standard hot cocoa mix, either from a packet or a large container. If you use a packet, use less than a full packet since the chocolate shell and extras will make the drink extra sweet. If you're measuring it, use about a tablespoon per bomb. This creates a light, creamy hot cocoa everyone will enjoy.

Luxury Hot Cocoa Mixes/Drinking Chocolate: These cocoa mixes are usually made with grated or flaked real chocolate. Keep in mind that hot cocoa mixes made with real chocolate may leave you with a bit of a grainy hot chocolate since it takes a very high temperature to melt the grated chocolate that powdered cocoa doesn't need. When using a luxury cocoa mix with real chocolate, I recommend microwaving your cocoa for an additional 20 seconds (after adding the cocoa bomb), and stirring extra well.

White Hot Cocoa Mix: White hot cocoa mix can be extra sweet when added to a chocolate bomb, so use a bit less than standard cocoa mix. Milk gets sweet when heated, so you may also want to try using hot water instead of milk, depending on how sweet you like your hot cocoa!

Chai, Cappuccino, or Other Prepared Drink Mixes: Prepared drink mixes are a great way to get unique or seasonal flavors such as chai, peppermint latte, or a pumpkin spice cappuccino. Use about half the amount that the package suggests for each 8-ounce cup per cocoa bomb.

Marshmallows: There used to just be . . . marshmallows. White fluffy barrels, available in regular for s'mores and mini for hot chocolate. Those were your choices. Nowadays, there is an entire shelf dedicated to marshmallows near the baking section: jumbo, colored, flavored, coated, twirled, stuffed, and in every shape you can imagine. There are keto-friendly, sugar-free, and vegan marshmallows. There are gourmet, handmade square marshmallows that are made for snacking, six-inch-long marshmallows made for stirring, and tiny dehydrated marshmallows like you would find in your hot cocoa packet. You can even buy the magical tiny colored marshmallows that used to be strictly in sugary breakfast cereals.

This marshmallow world is your playground! Feel free to swap out marshmallows as you see fit; there are no right or wrong marshmallows for each recipe, only ideas. If you happen to be one of the people who do not like marshmallows, don't fret! They are not necessary to any of the recipes (except perhaps the s'mores hot cocoa bomb!), so feel free to leave them out. I've seen tiny meringues that would make a fun alternative, or any mini cookie or candy you can find that works flavor-wise. Be creative!

Candy, Cookies, and More: Candy and mini cookies make great additions to hot cocoa bombs to mix things up instead of just hot cocoa mix, marshmallows, and sprinkles. There's an endless combination of flavor ideas to be had from the candy and cookie aisles. Also stroll the grab-and-go section, particularly of gas station convenience stores, to get ideas for unique items to add. Mini cookies and candies are sold in small packages here, and you can find other interesting new things, such as edible cookie dough bites, cupcake-flavored candy bites, granola bites, chocolate-covered nuts and fruits, and more.

The baking aisle also has plenty of great additions. Every possible flavor of baking chip can be found now, along with cookie crumbs, flavor crystals, dehydrated or freeze-dried ingredients, and more. You'll just want to be sure that whatever items you add will either dissolve nicely or remain whole long enough for you to grab them and eat them after they've been dunked in the hot cocoa. Try not to add items that will sink; the main fun is seeing what's inside rise to the surface, and items that sink may pose more of a choking risk.

*BE VERY CAREFUL to avoid choking hazards! For instance, do not add a whole round pep-permint or other candy, nuts, etc.; crush or chop it for safety. Make sure all who enjoy your hot cocoa bombs, and most especially children, are aware that some items such as harder sprinkles or candies may not fully dissolve and they should be extremely careful.

Freeze-Dried Fruit, Flavor Powders, and More

When making hot cocoa bombs, you'll need to use freeze-dried fruits instead of regular dried fruit. Regular dried fruit is exceedingly sweet, remains hard, and does not add much flavor when added to milk. It also releases moisture that will cause the hot cocoa mix to clump. Freeze-dried fruits are great additions for flavor, color, and texture, and come back to life extremely well in the hot milk. It's almost magical! Look for more unusual fruits, such as freeze-dried mango, watermelon, pineapple, fuji apple, or black currants. These are often found in the snack aisle by the nuts.

Speaking of nuts, they can add great flavor, but are not safe to add whole as you don't want them to become a choking hazard. Adding ground nuts is difficult because when ground they become oily, which can cause the cocoa mix to clump, and they also don't dissolve well. Peanut butter powder works well mixed with hot cocoa mix in some recipes. You can also use a scoop of actual peanut butter or hazelnut-chocolate butter, in much the same way you'd use ganache, without adding a dry mix.

Health powders, such as spirulina, dragonfruit powder, beet powder, matcha, maca, and others, can be added in small doses for color, flavor, and health benefits. When experimenting, be sure to consider that these powders not only add color, but also flavor, unlike powdered food colorings which simply add color. Adding matcha to make green may seem like a great idea, but only if you want matcha flavoring, which can be overpowering.

TECHNIQUES AND TIPS

Tempering Chocolate

What is tempering chocolate? Tempering chocolate is a way of heating, cooling, and repeating this process to get the molecules in the chocolate to behave in a certain way. It sounds silly, but that's the simplest way to describe it. When chocolate is not "in temper" as they say, the molecules are more random, and your chocolate will "bloom" (get a gray film that is the cocoa butter or sugar rising), soften at room temperature, and otherwise not behave. Tempered chocolate is glossy, shiny, and hard, creating that beautiful coating we all admire and that wonderful snap when you bite into a well-made chocolate. Tempering is simply adjusting the temperature a few times to get the chocolate into a perfect, beautiful condition for chocolate-making. However, it can be tricky, requires patience, and will likely take a few tries to get right. It might test *your* temper to get the chocolate in temper! But the results will be worth it, and it's a skill worth adding to your repertoire!

As previously mentioned, any "real" chocolate, that is, one that is not specifically a candy coating, will need to be tempered. To find out if you need to temper your chocolate, just look at the ingredients. Do you see "cocoa butter" listed? If so, you'll need to temper the chocolate.

When beginning to temper chocolate, you'll want to make sure all of your bowls and utensils are absolutely perfectly dry and do not have any droplets of water. Water will "break" or "seize" the chocolate, which means it ruins the emulsification. The entire batch will have to be thrown away (so sad!). Water is chocolate's enemy (one of many, unfortunately). Make sure you never heat the chocolate too quickly, as chocolate can easily scorch, and even the tiniest scorch will ruin your entire batch of chocolate. When stirring your chocolate, make sure you aren't whipping it in a circular motion which incorporates air. Instead, stir it in a figure-eight motion, switching directions north to south and east to west, so you aren't incorporating too much air but are still moving all of the chocolate. Tapping the filled molds before letting them set can release any trapped air bubbles.

There are many techniques for tempering chocolate, so feel free to try a few and pick your favorite. Don't give up if your chocolate doesn't temper perfectly the first time, if it takes a long time, or you have to start over. Tempering chocolate is a skill, and it's the reason there are high-end chocolate shops! But it *is* a skill the home chocolatier can master. Start with dark chocolate, as it is generally the easiest to temper. White chocolate is the most difficult to achieve a perfect temper. The microwave method may seem the most enticing, but it can also go awry rather easily, as microwaves are all different and are entirely unpredictable. If you do use the microwave method, be sure to use a microwave-safe *plastic* bowl as glass will hold too much heat and could easily overheat your chocolate even once you've taken it out of the microwave.

I asked my friend and owner of Four Brothers Chocolates in Glen Ellyn, Illinois, John Houlihan, to give us some tips on tempering chocolate at home, which I've incorporated here. "You can use the double-boiler method to temper chocolate very easily at home. I use chocolate from Guittard, one of the largest American manufacturers of chocolate. We use their couverture chocolate; that's the French word for 'covering.' It's basically any chocolate that has higher cocoa and butterfat and lends itself to a smoother, tastier, more wonderful end-product." John recommends the stovetop double-boiler method for home tempering, but admits the microwave tempering method can work, too. It's best to work with a larger amount of chocolate, at least one pound, regardless of method. Either way, he uses a simple ratio to know how much chocolate to melt at first and how much to reserve: "What I do is I have a little ratio that I use to help me figure out exactly what I need to temper. **Milk chocolate or white chocolate have the same characteristics, so you'll use 2 parts melted chocolate to 1 part solid chocolate. For dark chocolate, use a 3 to 1 ratio.**" This ratio is for what is called the "seeding method" and both of the methods below use the seeding method of tempering chocolate. This will make sense when you read the instructions below.

Seeding Method Ratios		
Milk or white chocolate	2 parts melted chocolate	1 part solid chocolate
Dark chocolate	3 parts melted chocolate	1 part solid chocolate

Stovetop/Double-Boiler "Seeding" Tempering Method

Finely chop at least 1 pound of chocolate. This will be the total amount you use and have tempered, and you'll divide it into the ratio mentioned above. Start with your total amount of chocolate you'd like to temper, and finely chop it. Then divide it according to the ratio above, and add the part that will be melted to the upper bowl of your double boiler. Add 2 inches of water to the bottom of the double boiler, add the upper bowl, and stir the chocolate as you bring the water to a simmer. Use a thermometer to keep an eye on the temperature the entire time, and remember to slowly stir. Let the chocolate fully melt and get to a temperature of around 105°F for white or milk chocolate and 115°F for dark chocolate. Do not exceed 120°F. Remove the top of the double boiler and safely set it on a heat-proof surface. Continue stirring, and add the reserved portion of chocolate a few small pieces at a time, waiting until each addition is fully melted, before adding more. Wait for the temperature to fall to 82°F. Then return your bowl to the top of the double boiler and heat the chocolate until it is 86–88°F. for milk or white chocolate, and 89–92°F for dark chocolate. Your chocolate should now be "in temper" and it's time to test it and make sure! Put a piece of wax paper or foil next to your double boiler and add a thin swipe of chocolate. Set this sample in the fridge for 3 minutes. Keep the rest of the chocolate on the heat and monitor the temp, stirring and removing from the heat as necessary to maintain the temperature, for the 3 minutes, so you don't lose the temper while you're testing. Keep stirring it; even if there's no heat, make sure the crystals are still moving around, for the 3 minutes. Then take your sample out. Does it look shiny? Does it snap in half? If so, your chocolate is tempered! If not, unfortunately, you'll have to start the process over.

Microwave "Seeding" Tempering Method

Finely chop at least 1 pound of chocolate. This will be the total amount you use and have tempered, and you'll divide it into the ratio mentioned above. Start with your total amount of chocolate you'd like to temper, and finely chop it. Then divide it according to the ratio above, and add the part that will be melted to your microwave-safe plastic bowl. Microwave no more than 30 seconds at a time, and stir thoroughly and test the temperature every 30 seconds. When the chocolate is becoming liquid, switch to 15-second intervals and use a thermometer to check the temperature after every 15 seconds (do *not* put the thermometer in the microwave!). Let the chocolate fully melt and get to a temperature of around 105°F for white or milk chocolate and 115°F for dark chocolate. Do not exceed 120°F. Remove the bowl and set it on a heat-proof surface. Continue stirring, and add the reserved portion of chocolate a few small pieces at a time, waiting until each addition is fully melted, before adding more. Wait for the temperature to fall to 82°F. Then return your bowl to the microwave and heat in 15-second intervals until the chocolate is at 86–88°F. for milk or white chocolate, and 89–92°F for dark chocolate. Your chocolate should now be "in temper" and it's time to test it and make sure! Put a piece of wax paper or foil next to your bowl and add a thin swipe of chocolate to it. Set this sample in the fridge for 3 minutes. Keep the rest of the chocolate warm, slowly stirring, and monitor the temperature, microwaving again for 10–15 seconds if necessary, so you don't lose the temper while you're testing. Keep stirring it, making sure the crystals are still moving around, for the 3 minutes. Then take your sample out. Does it look shiny? Does it snap in half? If so, your chocolate is tempered! If not, unfortunately, you'll have to start the process over.

Your first few attempts might not work perfectly, but keep trying. "Properly tempered chocolate will look beautiful, with a high-gloss and a perfect shine. It should have a very strong snap to it, a great sound when you break it. It shouldn't crumble, shouldn't have streaks, and will have a great mouth-feel," John says with enthusiasm. He and his team temper hundreds of pounds of chocolate by hand and he is confident the home chocolatier can create this beautiful result.

Can you reuse chocolate that didn't temper properly?

If the chocolate has broken, seized, or gotten above 120°F at any point, it's useless, and will not retemper. It will also likely have a grainy/gritty texture, as the actual ingredients of the chocolate have separated. Don't try to reuse the chocolate—just toss it. But if your chocolate has just gone out of temper—that is, you left it to cool too long—you can let it solidify and then try starting the tempering process over from scratch. Re-tempering chocolate that has gone out of temper will most likley work, but it's not guaranteed; since the chocolate has already been worked once, it may be more difficult the second time around.

Using Candy Melts

Candy melts that don't need to be tempered are perfect for beginners, kids, teens, and anyone who likes immediate gratification! Grab a bag of candy melts, melt them, and fill your molds! Candy melts will melt quickly in the microwave, if you choose to microwave them. Go very slowly at first and only in 30-second intervals, stirring between each round, moving to 10-second intervals once the chocolate is nearly melted. Even if the chocolate is still holding its shape and you think it needs longer, take it out and stir it! This type of chocolate is deceptive and will outwardly hold its shape even when it is soft inside, so be sure to stir it each time so the bottom chocolate doesn't burn and the temperature remains even throughout. If it is mostly melted, let the residual heat melt the last few pieces, as a thicker chocolate will be easier to keep up the sides of the molds and you won't risk overheating. Do not over-heat candy melts or you'll end up with streaky, powdery spots on your shells and they will be brittle since the candy will have separated.

CREATING THE CHOCOLATE SPHERES

Once you have melted chocolate, either tempered or candy melts, it's time to pour it into the molds.

Candy melts harden within minutes, so you'll want to work extra quickly when using those. A plastic-bristle, food-safe brush or the back of a small spoon (I like to use a measuring spoon) is best for coating the molds. Pour about 1 to 2 tablespoons into each mold, and use the spoon and brush to make sure it coats the sides all the way to the top. Don't work in big batches or you'll end up with a few molds that have hardened blobs in them before you can bring the chocolate up the edges!

If you're using polycarbonate molds, the professional way to get perfect shapes is to fill each mold cavity entirely to the top, and fill as many cavities as you can, then swirl and tap the chocolate in the molds. Turn it upside down over the bowl and let all of the extra chocolate flow out, switching the direction you're letting it run from horizontally to vertically. Use your bench scraper to scrape all the extra chocolate from the tops and sides of the mold into the bowl. Repeat if necessary to fill all of the molds.

Some chocolates will tend to fall back to the center, resulting in very thin, fragile edges and a thick top/bottom that won't melt with the heat of the milk poured over it. After the first 5 minutes in the refrigerator, use your brush or back of the spoon to either take extra not-set chocolate from the bottom of the mold up around the edges, or use extra chocolate to carefully spoon/brush up the edges. Refrigerate again. Make sure you don't make the bottom too thin; you don't want to see any of the mold showing through.

Carefully place the molds in the refrigerator for 5 minutes to fully harden. I like to let them come back to room temperature before popping them from the molds as I feel they are brittle while still cold and the edges are more prone to cracking. Be sure to have cold hands when removing the chocolate, and/or wear chocolate gloves, to ensure you don't leave smudgy, melty fingerprints on the chocolate.

Don't leave the filled molds in the refrigerator (or freezer, if you're just trying to get them to pop out of polycarbonate molds) too long or they will get condensation on them. Remember the rule that water is chocolate's enemy? Your chocolate will be ruined if you leave it in the refrigerator or freezer too long in the mold.

If you're using polycarbonate molds, checking the bottom can help you determine if the chocolate is fully set. Carefully lift it up and check the bottom of the mold. Still-wet chocolate will be darker and look stuck to the bottom of the mold. When the chocolate is fully set, it will be lighter and look lifted away slightly. To release the chocolate half spheres from polycarbonate molds, simply use one finger to lift the inside of the cup up and out to the side. It should come away naturally, as when the chocolate hardens it shrinks slightly, releasing it from the mold. If it needs a bit of help, pop it in the freezer for 5–10 minutes.

If you're using silicone molds, be careful how/where you set the molds before they are fully set as you can indent them and that will show in the final half sphere. Be careful when releasing the chocolates from the silicone molds as they can quickly flip inside out if you aren't careful and throw the chocolate across the room! I've even had them flip across the counter into the dirty dish water, which is sad indeed! You'll want to start very carefully peeling the edges away and down, pushing gently on the bottom of the mold to push it inside out and release the half sphere. Do one at a time, carefully. A trick to make this easier: You can cut your mold into single cups and place them on a baking tray before filling. Then you can release them one half sphere at a time, without risk of damaging them all.

Once fully hardened, the empty chocolate half spheres can be stored at room temperature for up to 2 weeks, or 4 weeks in an airtight container. I've found the easiest way to store these is in a cupcake carrier. The cupcake molds are the perfect size and a carrier holds plenty. You can also stack the half spheres as they are solid and shouldn't melt or stick as long as they are kept in a cool, dry place. However, they will scratch each other if the edges drag along the top or side of another half-sphere. You can place muffin liners under each half sphere to prevent this, or if the spheres contain coloring or flavoring that you don't want to transfer.

FILLING THE SPHERES

Once you have your finished half spheres, you can immediately fill them or keep them in an airtight container for up to two weeks as is. Remember, you'll only fill half the spheres, as the other half will be the tops,

so be sure to set aside half before you start. In order to get a straight, tight seal, you'll want to melt the edges of both half-spheres. That means you'll need to melt/straighten the edges of the bottom halves you'll be filling *before* you fill them. To do so, place a non-stick or aluminum skillet on the stovetop over very low heat. Very gently and quickly place the edges of the cocoa bomb on the hot pan for a few seconds until the edges are melted evenly all around. Do this quickly and do not let too much of the edges melt or the spheres will not be the same size. Turn the burner off while you fill the bottom halves. It's okay if the edges of the bottom halves set; the goal is only to create an even, flat surface for the top edge to adhere to.

If you've made a "recipe batch" of either the regular hot cocoa mix or the white hot cocoa mix (pages 40 and 41), use 1 heaping tablespoon per cocoa bomb. If you're using a store bought mix, use approximately half the suggested amount for one 8-ounce serving.

You might think there's not much room left, but remember, you have the entire height of the top globe to work with as well, so feel free to pile as high as you can! Add color powders to the dry mixture before adding any other items to ensure it will be properly mixed.

Do *not* add any items that are not fully dry or that contain moisture that will potentially soften the chocolate, make the dry mix clump, or, worst of all, allow mold growth. Regular marshmallows and cookies do contain slight moisture, so I recommend using those cocoa bombs within a week. If you use dehydrated marshmallows, your cocoa bombs will be shelf stable longer, at least two weeks. Also think of shelf life and stability when adding things like pretzels or cookies that could go stale and ruin the taste. Just make sure to use these cocoa bombs more quickly.

ATTACHING THE SPHERES

The most common and practical way to attach the sphere is to melt the edges lightly and press them together. Don't worry if your cocoa bomb edges are not perfect. You'll see many in here that are not, and they work just fine! For even edges and a tight seal, you'll want to melt the edges of *both* half spheres, as mentioned. Repeat the process above, using a wide, shallow pan on very low heat, and gently and quickly place the edges of the sphere flat against the pan to melt them evenly. Then quickly and carefully press the two half sphere edges together. If you've accidentally melted one sphere too much, they may not fit on top of each other, but rather inside of each other. This is fine; it won't create a perfectly round sphere but it will taste just as delicious!

If there is excess melted chocolate around the seal, use your finger or a brush to fill it into any gaps that might remain or to gently smooth it. Sometimes I think it leaves a neater finish to leave it as is if there isn't much chocolate, because using your finger to smooth it will leave marks. If any small gaps remain in the edge seal, fill them in by using a brush with the chocolate that has melted in the pan. Leaving even the smallest gap means cocoa powder will spill out any time you move these! Let the spheres completely dry before moving them to ensure the seal remains tight.

DECORATING

Here comes the fun part: Decorating! Of course hot cocoa bombs can transform into any manner of themes with the addition of some simple decorating techniques. Don't go overboard, though: keep in mind the decorations and chocolate shell need to be restrained enough to still allow only a few ounces of hot milk to melt them. A half-melted hot chocolate bomb is a sad sight indeed, much less amusing than the fun of a lightweight chocolate ball that floats, bobs, and dissolves into deliciousness.

Luster/Shimmer/Color Powders

There are different kinds of powders you might use to add depth, shine, and glitter to your cocoa bomb exteriors. From frosted-shine luster powder to disco-ball-glitter powder, to simple colored powders, the variety is huge. Just make absolutely sure you're using an edible glitter/powder, as an online search often throws craft glitter into the results, and that's not a mistake you'd want to eat!

Some recipes will call for a bit of decorating *before* pouring the chocolate into the mold. This is likely to be luster or color powders. Simply use a full brush, such as a brand-new and washed and dried face powder brush or specially-designed cake powder brush. Make sure your brush is absolutely and completely dry! Dip the brush lightly into the coating (I like to tap a bit of the color powder into the lid, then swirl my brush around the lid). Lightly sweep the brush in circular motions to fully coat the inside of your mold, tapping any excess powder out by turning over the mold.

You'll also likely add extra powder after the shells have set and been unmolded. Use the same brush, and use swirling motions to cover evenly. These powders come in varying levels of luster/shine, so use them with care and remember you will be eating these, so don't go overboard!

Edible Glitter/Metallic Flakes/Etc.

Edible glitter is luster powder's big sister, and she knows how to glam up! This glitter looks and acts like real glitter, but is edible (make *sure* you get the edible version!). Use it carefully! I like to either add a tiny bit to the dry mixture to create a surprise sparkly drink *or* dust a small amount on top of the finished cocoa bomb. You can also dip items in the glitter and add them on top using edible glue or melted chocolate to adhere. Edible glitter can be a bit expensive, but the reaction you'll get to the dazzling effect will be well worth the investment.

Metallic flakes and shapes are fun, too, and come in gold, silver, copper, and rose gold. These are not always true gold or silver, but create a fantastic effect on top of cocoa bombs. Depending on the style, they may be flakes, shards, or shaped. They may need a bit of edible glue to adhere, depending on how you are using them.

I also found metallic edible sequins, imported from England, which are utterly fantastic and unique. There are shimmery sprinkles that look like fresh-water pearls and make a perfect addition to any water- or mermaid-themed cocoa bomb. There are gilded roses and rose petals for an elegant touch, or even gilded sugar rocks that look like geodes. The possibilities are nearly endless.

Edible Gold and Silver Leaf

Edible gold and silver leaf are thinner-than-paper sheets of actual gold and silver that are deemed pure enough to be edible. Once again, you'll want to use this delicate decoration in small amounts, remembering that it will be ingested. However, it is undeniably the fanciest topper for a cocoa bomb, hands down. I don't recommend adding this to the interior of the cocoa bomb, but instead let it shine on top in all of its gold or silver stunningness. Use a brush or delicate tweezers to gently lift the metallic

leaf off the paper it comes on, and place gently on the surface. You don't need anything to adhere it; it will naturally adhere. Be sure you order edible-grade gold leaf and not artist-grade gold leaf, then gild away!

Candy Melts

Candy melts are the obvious choice for decorating as they offer fun colors and there's no need to temper decorating chocolate. Simply melt, fill a small pastry bag, and pipe back and forth for intriguing lines, or make circular motions for a lovely flowery effect. Of course, it can get much more detailed than this, but that's all that's needed to create a professional-looking hot cocoa bomb. You can even buy pre-made pouches of candy melts just for decorating, in just the right amount to dress up a batch of bombs.

Think about using coordinating colors to the flavors, an ombré version of the colors used to make the bomb, or even a complementary color from that color wheel . . . remember in elementary school? Complementary colors are the colors opposite each other on the color wheel and instantly make pleasing combinations, because they, well, complement one another. For instance, orange and blue, red and green, or purple and yellow are complementary colors and look great together.

Isomalt Shapes

Edible gems that look like true rubies, sapphires, and diamonds? Welcome to the world of isomalt shapes! Isomalt is a sugar alcohol (a sugar substitute) that is clear and creates transparent hard candies with the glimmer of real gems. These are fantastic additions to the exterior of cocoa bombs (or interior if used with extreme caution due to them being a potential choking hazard) that really elevate your cocoa bomb style. Look for these in cake decorating stores, on specialty cake-decorating websites, or on Etsy. You can also find isomalt translucent decorations in nearly every shape, including fire flames and water-style decorations that are next-level for decorating!

Fondant/Marzipan Decorations

Fondant is an edible icing "clay" that is made from sugar, water, and corn syrup, and it sometimes has glycerin or gelatin added. Since fondant can be worked like clay, it is possible to create incredibly detailed figures that are three-dimensional as well. Decorations can be in any shape and style, but creating them is an art form unto itself! I love to purchase specialty fondant decorations or characters from artisans on Etsy. You can also purchase plain and colored fondant in most cake- and candy-making aisles and play around. Gel food coloring or powdered food coloring is usually added to color white fondant. There are specialty fondant-working tools and mats, but you can make do with a silicone mat from your kitchen and various kitchen implements. Fondant decorations are semi-soft but harden with age. Do not try to eat hardened fondant decorations; you might lose a tooth!

Marzipan is similar to fondant in that it is a paste-type filling or edible "clay" that is made from sugar or honey, egg whites, and almond flour, giving it an almond flavor and a slightly gritty texture. It can be shaped and colored just like fondant, and perhaps more delicately since it has a unique texture. It is often shaped into fruits, vegetables, or animals and sold in bakeries, particularly around the holidays. To create your own marzipan shapes, find a tube of marzipan in the baking aisle (for some reason, it's usually on the top shelf). Don't confuse marzipan for almond paste; they are different and almond paste will not sculpt and stay like marzipan. Powdered food colorings with a delicate brush color marzipan nicely. Marzipan also hardens completely over time and becomes inedible.

Sprinkles

You might be used to only two options for sprinkles: rainbow or chocolate. This is just the very beginning of the sprinkle spectrum nowadays. You can find nearly every color, shape, size, and theme you can imagine in sprinkle form. They may be hard sugar, colored sugar, or fondant, and may or may not dissolve in your hot milk. Craft stores have a great selection; indeed, even your local grocery store likely has a few unique blends. There are also several online stores that have made a business out of creative, jazzy blends with names to match. Etsy is another great place for unique sprinkles, sprinkle mixes, and fondant fillers or items. If you can think of an item, type into your search engine and add "sprinkles" after it . . . I bet you'll find something! Believe it or not, you'll want to make sure you're getting edible sprinkles, as many are made from clay and are not actually edible.

You will also find some extremely metallic sprinkles out there that really look like real metal. However, I have not included these in the book as they are not yet FDA-approved. While they are approved by the similar governing bodies of other countries, I urge you to use caution and use these only for decorating if you must.

*Again, please be aware that some larger and harder sprinkles pose a choking hazard and require great care and caution.

Stirrers

Cocoa bombs do need to be stirred more than standard hot cocoa mix, to ensure the chocolate shell is melted and all of the ingredients are properly mixed. Why use just a spoon? Stirrers can be a fun part of the decorating and packaging process. Of course, candy canes, old-fashioned penny-candy sticks, and rock candy sticks are easy additions. But think outside the box for stirrers, too! Sturdy licorice with a hole through the center makes a fun straw. Honey sticks or spoons add a delicious honey flavor. Spoons made out of cookies (you can buy these or find a mold online to use for baking your own) or chocolate (also use a mold for these) are sweet additions. Pretzel rods add a bit of salt to some of the more sweet-and-salty flavor combinations. Six-inch marshmallows are great to stir and then melt into the cocoa.

Everything Else You Can Possibly Imagine

The world of candy and edible decorations is virtually limitless. If you're thinking of something unique, perhaps, say, lace, and how you could incorporate it into your cocoa bomb, simply search "edible lace." You'll find all sorts of beautiful sugar lace, from classic white to metallic gold. Gilded rose petals? Leaves? Butterflies? Your own face? These can all be created from rice paper that is printed (literally on a printer) with edible ink and cut to shapes that can even be three-dimensional. The leaves on the Pumpkin Spice Cocoa Bombs (page 47) are edible rice paper decorations. There are edible pens and markers you can use to create detailed designs, regular and metallic edible paint to make a plain cocoa bomb your canvas, gum paste flowers, flavored isomalt crystals, edible geodes, 3-D eyeballs that look almost too real to eat, delicate edible feathers, and freeze-dried cakes and pies. If you can imagine it, chances are, you can find it in edible form to add to your cocoa bombs.

Edible "Glue" for Attaching Items

Now, when it comes to attaching "everything you can possibly imagine" it can be a bit of a trick on a round, slick chocolate surface. Enter edible glue! Edible glue, used by chocolatiers and cake makers, can be useful in attaching all manner of decorations to finished cocoa bombs. There are many different types of edible glue that can be purchased, usually made with Tylose or Gum Paste. You can purchase each of these ingredients from specialty shops and make your own edible glue that won't harden immediately if you'd like, or simply purchase a pre-made glue. They generally come in bottles with droppers or brushes attached for convenience. If not, grab your own clean, small brush. Edible glue is fantastic *but* it does take a long time to dry, and items may shift or fall off during this time. Edible glue is best used for light items (such as rice paper decorations or large areas of sprinkles).

You can also make your own version of an edible sugar "glue" by heating about a cup of sugar until it is fully melted and caramelized but not burnt, then letting it cool slightly (so it won't melt your cocoa bomb) but not harden before using. This will harden rather quickly, though, so you'll need to make a new batch each time you need it.

Using extra melted chocolate, usually whatever I have left around, is actually my favorite way to attach extras, especially heavy ones. Dip the item in the chocolate, hold it gently in place for a solid 30 seconds while pressing gently but firmly (and not on a seam!), then put it in the refrigerator immediately for at least 5 minutes. It's not fool-proof (see my sleepy unicorn ear on page 166), but it keeps things in place.

Another way to get things to stay is to heat the cocoa bomb itself very, very gently by quickly using a kitchen/crème brûlée torch. This one works great when you don't want any melted chocolate or glue to show, but must be done with extreme caution because it can melt a hole within a split second! Gently melt the area with your torch just barely, then add your sprinkles or topping. I may or may not have set the edible flowers on fire for the Honey-Lovin' Cocoa Bomb (page 151), so again, I urge you to use caution.

For glitter or any other powder topping, my favorite way to attach those powders is to use a thick, flat brush just barely dipped in vegetable oil, soft coconut oil, or shortening and paint where I want to add the glitter. Make sure you completely cover the "wet" area or it will remain that way and may be slippery!

TROUBLESHOOTING

The goal is shiny, perfectly shaped cocoa bombs, but chocolate isn't always the easiest to work with. Overheating is the most common problem, so be sure to heat your chocolate slow and steady, no matter what kind you're using.

My Chocolate Won't Set!

What kind of chocolate are you using? Make sure you are using chocolate that can melt and set again. Chocolate chips will not work, sadly. Some white chocolates, even in bar form, are just difficult and won't work, either. If your chocolate won't/hasn't set, unfortunately there's no way to remedy this and you'll have to start over. Try using candy melts or a different brand of chocolate.

I Can't Get My Chocolate Out of the Mold!

Uh-oh! Did water get into your chocolate somehow? Did you leave it in the refrigerator or freezer too long? If not, try popping the mold into the freezer for 5 minutes. If that doesn't work, you may have used the incorrect chocolate or it wasn't fully tempered, and now you'll just have to scrape or wash it out and start over.

My Cocoa Bomb Edges Are Too Brittle!

This is a common problem, and using a brush to make sure the chocolate gets all the way to the top of the mold is helpful. Make sure you get at least two layers of chocolate on the edges before the chocolate fully solidifies. Also make sure you haven't overheated your chocolate as the separation will make it brittle.

My Chocolate Is Streaky or Swirly!

If your finished cocoa bombs have white spots or are streaky, it's likely that your chocolate "broke," which means separated, probably from overheating. This won't hurt you and will likely taste and work fine, but chances are it is more brittle. Try again and watch your heat carefully.

My Cocoa Bomb Edges Won't Stick Together!

If your cocoa bomb edges are not staying stuck together, you might not be letting the chocolate on the edges melt long enough to create a flat edge. Be sure to do this on both half-spheres.

My Finished Cocoa Bomb Is Melting!

First of all, it's not in a warm place, near the stove, or in a sunny window, right? If not, chances are your chocolate was not properly tempered or was too thin.

My Finished Cocoa Bomb Is Turning White or Gray!

This gray or white film on chocolate is called "bloom" and is the fat or sugar separating and rising to the exterior. It is caused by improper tempering or by using the wrong kind of chocolate. But don't worry, it does not affect taste and is fine to eat.

STORAGE/GIFTING/PACKAGING

Hot chocolate bombs are an elegant gift for nearly any occasion. They can be thoroughly personalized. One alone is an indulgent special treat; a half-dozen is a truly decadent gift. Two for a couple makes a thoughtful anniversary gift, a birthday hot chocolate bomb personalized with the recipient's favorite colors and initial is sure to impress, and someone under the weather will be grateful for a superfood or get-well-soon chocolate bomb that not only helps them get back on their feet but makes them forget their worries for a few moments. Hot chocolate bombs can be rather fragile, though, as they are indeed hollow, so you'll need to keep that in mind when gifting and packaging.

Storage

How long do the shells last unfilled? The unfilled, undecorated shells will last in an airtight container for up to 4 weeks.

Do I need to refrigerate the finished cocoa bombs? In general, no. Most recipes in this book are shelf-stable if made as directed. If they need to be refrigerated when made as directed, the recipe will explicitly state this. If you add any extra ingredients or aren't sure, please refrigerate for food safety.

How long do finished cocoa bombs last? Most filled cocoa bombs will last at least 2 weeks if left in a cool, dry place and if they do not contain any moisture-creating ingredients. If they contain regular marshmallows instead of dehydrated marshmallows, or any cookies or freeze-dried cake that could become stale, it's best to use them within 1 week.

Packaging

Cocoa bombs are such fun to gift, I have a feeling you'll be giving a lot of them to friends and neighbors! Presentation is a huge part of the appeal of cocoa bombs, so packaging is as important as decorating if you're giving these away (though no one will turn one away even if it isn't fancily packaged!).

The options for packaging are nearly endless, but here are some of my favorites and some creative options:

- Berry Baskets (paper, plastic, or ceramic)
- Egg Cartons (EggCartons.com makes a single Kraft carton specifically designed for cocoa bombs! Smaller bombs fit in regular-size cartons.)
- Clear or metallic "painter's cans/pails"
- Miniature jars with wide mouths
- Cupcake boxes with inserts
- Clear plastic, paper, or acrylic cocoa bomb boxes
- Clear plastic or acrylic tubes
- Mugs or teacups, of course!
- Miniature cast iron pans (as seen in S'mores recipe, page 45)
- Spoon rests (These can be the perfect round size and also offer a place to put your spoon or stirrer, or any larger candies.)
- Vintage butter pats or lonely saucers left from broken teacups (Check your local thrift store! Mine has a stack of gorgeously gilded single saucers for a quarter each.)
- Pillar candle stands
- Cupcake stands
- Mason jar lids, new or vintage (line vintage lids first)
- Cupcake liners (Don't be shy about layering them! The more the merrier!)
- Pretty drink coasters
- Vintage tins from candies, cocoa, etc. (My thrift store has a giant bin of these for $1 each and they are so pretty!)
- Clear plastic bags tied with ribbon or a card topper stapled on top
- Ring/trinket dishes
- Miniature pails/buckets

- Silicone cupcake liners
- Raw wood slices
- Paper ice cream/treat cups
- Mini takeout containers
- Ramekins or small bowls

Please make sure your surfaces are food-safe if the cocoa bomb will be touching them directly. Otherwise, be sure to line the surface with waxed paper, parchment paper, a cupcake liner, foil, a paper doily, or something else food-safe!

You might also need some "nesting" materials if your packaging doesn't have a cupcake-style insert or strong enough base to keep your cocoa bomb stable.

- Edible grass (usually sold around Easter and comes in many colors)
- Crinkle paper shreds
- Plenty of extra marshmallow "pillows"
- Use a dab of frosting, melted chocolate, or edible glue on the bottom of your cocoa bomb to stick it to the packaging surface
- Paper doilies in all colors/shapes
- Tissue, parchment, or waxed paper (this may leave marks on a chocolate bomb if hard edges touch the chocolate)

Don't forget to package your cocoa bombs with extras to create a truly engaging gift! Extras can include:

- A special mug
- Spoon, mini whisk, stirrers, or mini spatula
- A small mallet to break the bomb open before putting in the mug
- Cookies, chocolates, or treats to enjoy with the cocoa
- A small bag of coffee if the cocoa bomb pairs well with coffee
- A special movie to watch or book to read
- A cozy blanket, scarf, or socks
- Small items for decorating a little "scene" around the mug of hot cocoa for social media photos, of course, including: LED string lights, a coaster, small sign, little figurine, etc.

If you're drooling at this point, and day-dreaming of hot cocoa while reading this, it's time to head to the kitchen! First we'll start with the basics of creating the interior cocoa mixes and the three types of basic chocolate bombs. Then we'll dive into the dozens of unique recipes that will hopefully start as a jumping off point for your own creations, too.

RECIPES

Hot Cocoa Mix

A lot of homemade hot cocoa mixes have powdered milk in them, and are made to be stirred into hot water. However, since we're adding hot milk here, and the bombs have limited space inside them that is much better filled with treats and surprises instead of powdered milk, this recipe leaves that out. With the addition of the chocolate cocoa shell adding richness, I promise you won't miss it one bit. If you do add powdered milk, I recommend seeking out whole milk powder as opposed to the standard non-fat milk found in the baking aisle. The difference is huge.

Single Serving: For one cocoa bomb. Use this recipe when you have some extra cocoa bomb shells hanging around or want to experiment with a new flavor combination. No need to whip up a huge batch; just get out your measuring spoons instead of measuring cups!

1½ teaspoons cocoa powder
1½ teaspoons sugar
A few grains of salt

Mix well and use to fill one cocoa bomb. Makes approximately 1 tablespoon of cocoa mix.

Recipe Batch: To make and fill any 6-bomb recipe in this book; double if making a double batch of a recipe; halve if making a half recipe.

4 tablespoons cocoa powder
4 tablespoons sugar
¼ teaspoon salt

Mix well. Use one tablespoon per serving. Fills 6 cocoa bombs with 1 tablespoon of mix each. Makes approximately ½ cup of cocoa mix.

Stock-Up Recipe: To fill the pretty jar on your counter and make a hot cocoa bomb, or recipe batch, any time instantly! Use the single serving amount or recipe amount (1 tablespoon for single or ½ cup for recipe batch).

2½ cups cocoa powder
2½ cups sugar
1 teaspoon salt

Mix well. Store in an airtight container.

White Hot Cocoa Mix

I tested and tasted nearly every variation of homemade white hot cocoa mix out there and none of them were up to par! Dry nonfat milk . . . blech. Dry plain creamer . . . no thanks. Pudding mix? I can't imagine drinking that. They all tasted powdery and slightly sour. I didn't need white chocolate chips because the shell is white chocolate. Enter Ghirardelli's Sweet White Ground powder. This white chocolate magic powder is specifically formulated to dissolve in milk. It creates the perfect white cocoa on its own, or you can dress it up. I like to add a pinch of salt and a dash of vanilla powder. Voilà. You may need to order the Ghirardelli powder online or find a specialty chocolate or coffee shop in your area that carries it, but it's worth it.

Single Serving: For one cocoa bomb. Use this recipe when you have some extra cocoa bomb shells hanging around or want to experiment with a new flavor combination. No need to whip up a huge batch, just get out your measuring spoons instead of cups!

1 tablespoon Ghirardelli Sweet White Ground powder
A few grains of salt
A dash of vanilla powder, if desired

Mix well and use to fill one cocoa bomb. Makes approximately one tablespoon of cocoa mix.

Recipe Servings: To make and fill any recipe in this book; double if making a double batch of a recipe; halve if making a half recipe!

½ cup Ghirardelli Sweet White Ground powder
1 teaspoon salt
1 tablespoon vanilla powder

Mix well. Use 1 tablespoon per serving. Fills 6 cocoa bombs with 1 tablespoon of mix each. Makes approximately ½ cup of cocoa mix.

Stock-Up Serving: To fill the pretty jar on your counter and make hot cocoa any time instantly! Use the single serving amount or recipe amount.

2 cups Ghirardelli Sweet White Ground powder
1 tablespoon salt
¼ cup vanilla powder

Mix well. Store in an airtight container.

Basic Cocoa Bomb Shells

Here is the basic procedure for creating 6 whole (12 half) cocoa bomb shells using a 2.5-inch mold. You'll need between 10 and 12 ounces of chocolate, as different chocolates and viscosities will make them more or less liquid, sturdy, etc. Use the full 12 ounces to be safe, until you know each different type of chocolate.

Start with 10–12 ounces of tempered milk, dark, or white chocolate, ready to use, or any flavor candy melts, melted. Pour or use a scoop to add about 1–2 tablespoons into each mold cavity.

Silicone molds: Use the back of a spoon or a plastic-bristle, food-only brush to bring the chocolate up the sides and to coat all the way to the top. It's easier to overfill and go over the edges than to underfill, since once you unmold them, the extra will likely fall right off. Don't work in big batches or you'll end up with a few molds that have hardened blobs in them before you can bring the chocolate up the edges! It is okay to re-melt the leftover candy melts in the microwave (in the bowl, *not* in the mold) if it hardens before you can fill all of the molds.

Polycarbonate molds: You can use the spoon/brush method above in polycarbonate molds, but the easier and professional way to get perfect shapes is to fill each mold cavity entirely to the top, and fill as many cavities as you can, then swirl and tap the chocolate in the molds. Turn the mold upside down over the bowl and let all of the extra chocolate flow out, switching the direction you're letting it run from horizontally to vertically. Use your bench scraper to scrape all the extra chocolate from the tops and sides of the mold into the bowl.

Next: Some chocolates will tend to fall back to the center, resulting in very thin, fragile edges and a thick top/bottom that won't melt with the heat of the milk poured over it. After the first 5 minutes in the refrigerator, use your brush or back of the spoon to either take extra not-set chocolate from the bottom of the mold up around the edges, or use extra chocolate to carefully spoon/brush up the edges. Refrigerate again. Make sure you don't make the bottom too thin; you don't want to see any of the mold showing through.

Carefully place the molds in the refrigerator for 5 minutes to fully harden. I like to let them come back to room temperature before popping them from the molds as I feel they are brittle while still cold and the edges are more prone to cracking. Be sure to have cold hands when removing the chocolate, and/or wear chocolate gloves, to ensure you don't leave smudgy, melty fingerprints on the chocolate.

S'mores Cocoa Bombs

This S'mores Cocoa Bomb is a night around the campfire in a mug. It will bring you right back to summer bonfires with your friends, and is perfect when the air starts to chill and you head indoors. To scorch the marshmallows, use a crème brûleée torch ever-so-carefully, because the torch will melt any chocolate it hits nearly instantly. If you don't have a crème brûlée torch, the only other method I recommend is toasting the marshmallow over another flame and then adding them to the cocoa bombs. Messy? Maybe. But that has always been part of the appeal of s'mores, right? For an extra special touch, pile on plenty more marshmallows once the cocoa bomb has melted, and torch those lightly (or thoroughly) too. Since they aren't on a chocolate shell, you can burn those to a crisp if you'd like! The mini cast iron pans (usually sold alongside the full-size ones in any camping store) really add to the whole outdoorsy appeal, as do metal or camp-inspired mugs.

Makes 6 regular or 10–12 mini cocoa bombs

- 12 ounces milk chocolate candy melts *or* milk chocolate, tempered
- 1 recipe batch hot cocoa mix (page 40) *or* ½ cup store-bought mix
- 1 cup chocolate chunks (such as for baking)
- 1½ cups mini marshmallows, plus more for decorating
- 1 cup mini graham cracker cookies or broken bits of graham cracker
- Edible glue or a bit of extra melted chocolate, for decorating
- Graham cracker cookies or broken bits of graham cracker, for decorating
- 6 milk chocolate round wafers or large squares, for decorating

To Make: Place a hot cocoa bomb with the freshly toasted marshmallows in the bottom of a mug. Add 8–10 ounces of very hot milk and stir well. Reheat in the microwave for approximately 20 seconds to thoroughly heat, and stir well again for best taste. Best enjoyed in front of a fireplace while playing charades with friends.

Melt the chocolate thoroughly. Pour 1–2 tablespoons of the melted chocolate into each mold and use a brush or the back of a spoon to make sure the chocolate fills in all of the mold and up the edges. Refrigerate 5 minutes to set. If the edges are thin, carefully brush more chocolate around the edges and refrigerate for 5 more minutes. Carefully unmold. Set aside 6 of the shells for the tops. Melt the edges of 6 of the shells that will be the bottoms. Fill these cocoa bomb shells with: 1 tablespoon hot cocoa mix, a handful of chocolate chunks, and a handful of mini marshmallows. Add mini graham cracker cookies or pieces to each of the bottom shells as well. Melt the edges of the leftover shells and attach the tops. Let set. To decorate, use a bit of edible glue or melted chocolate to attach a small square of graham cracker to the top of each cocoa bomb. Then use the edible glue or melted chocolate to attach a chocolate wafer or large piece of chocolate to the top of the graham cracker (carefully so it doesn't break!). Use a bit of edible glue or melted chocolate to attach a few mini marshmallows to the top. Repeat for all cocoa bombs. Let all dry thoroughly. Then, just before consuming, use a crème brûlée torch to lightly, quickly toast only the marshmallows.

Pumpkin Spice Cocoa Bombs

Oh pumpkin spice. How we love to love-hate you. Add it to chocolate, though, and I think we can all agree it's a fantastic way to celebrate fall. I used milk chocolate for a classic pumpkin spice hot cocoa, but dark chocolate works too. These are also delicious made in white chocolate cocoa bomb shells with white cocoa mix, where a bit more of the pumpkin part of the pumpkin spice flavoring comes through. If you don't have pumpkin spice flavoring oil, you can substitute 1 teaspoon of pumpkin spice powdered spice mix in the chocolate itself, but the flavor won't be as pronounced and won't have the "pumpkin" flavor.

MAKES 6 REGULAR COCOA BOMBS

12 ounces milk chocolate candy melts *or* milk chocolate, tempered *or* white candy melts *or* white chocolate, tempered

1 teaspoon pumpkin spice flavoring oil, to taste

1 recipe batch hot cocoa mix (page 40) *or* ½ cup store-bought mix

2 tablespoons pumpkin pie spice, plus more for decorating

½ cup mini marshmallows *or* pumpkin-shaped marshmallows

Edible glue or a bit of chocolate, melted, for decorating

Edible rice-paper fall leaves, for decorating

Melt the chocolate and thoroughly stir in the flavoring to taste. Refrigerate 5 minutes to set. If the edges are thin, carefully brush more chocolate around the edges and refrigerate for 5 more minutes. Carefully unmold. Set 6 shells aside for the tops. Melt the edges of the remaining 6 shells that will be the bottoms. Fill these shells with: 1 tablespoon cocoa mix, a pinch of pumpkin pie spice, and a handful of mini marshmallows. Melt the edges of the remaining shells and attach the tops. Let set. To decorate, brush a bit of edible glue or melted chocolate to the top of each bomb. Add a light sprinkle of pumpkin pie spice and one or two of the edible leaves.

To Make: Place a hot cocoa bomb in the bottom of a mug. Add 10 ounces of very hot milk and stir well. Reheat in the microwave for approximately 20 seconds to thoroughly heat, and stir well again for best taste. Now it's time to carve or decorate your pumpkins!

Caramel Apple Cocoa Bombs

These adorable cocoa bombs will have your mouth watering the moment you see them; they just scream fall fun! Charming enough as is, these are even more fun displayed in a wooden crate for a party or gift. I've filled them with white cocoa mix so you can really taste the apple, but they are delicious with regular cocoa, too. They've finally decided to create small, morsel-size caramel bits for baking and candy making, but if you can't find these, use a sharp knife lightly rubbed with vegetable oil to carefully cut soft caramels into pieces. For some reason, green apple flavoring oil may thicken your chocolate so don't go over ¼ teaspoon or you'll end up with play dough (and re-melting won't help).

MAKES 6 REGULAR COCOA BOMBS

8 ounces green candy melts *or* white chocolate, tempered, colored green

⅛–¼ teaspoon green apple flavoring oil

10 ounces caramel candy melts *or* white chocolate, tempered, colored caramel, divided

¼–½ teaspoon caramel flavoring oil

1 recipe batch white hot cocoa mix (page 41) *or* ½ cup store-bought mix

Caramel bits *or* unwrapped soft caramels, chopped

Freeze-dried apple, optional

½ cup dehydrated mini marshmallows

Clean, unused popsicle sticks, for decorating

Melt the green chocolate thoroughly. Add the green apple flavoring and work quickly to fill 6 molds, as the green apple flavoring may thicken the chocolate. Repeat with 8 ounces the caramel candy melts and add the caramel flavoring oil. Fill the remaining 6 molds. Refrigerate 5 minutes to set. Carefully unmold. Set aside the 6 caramel shells for the tops. Melt the edges of the 6 green shells that will be the bottoms. Fill these shells with: 1 tablespoon white cocoa mix, a handful of caramel bits, a few pieces of freeze-dried apple, and a handful of mini marshmallows. Melt the edges of the caramel shells and attach the tops. Let set. To decorate, use kitchen scissors to carefully cut the popsicle sticks in half so you have 6 halves. Melt the remaining caramel candy melts. Work on one cocoa bomb at a time. Dip the popsicle stick half in the caramel and gather a liberal amount on the end, then swirl the extra into a circle on top of the cocoa bomb and stand the stick in the center. Hold steady for at least 30 seconds until the stick will stay upright, then immediately refrigerate for 5 minutes. Repeat for the remaining cocoa bombs.

To Make: Place a hot cocoa bomb in the bottom of a mug. Add 8–10 ounces of very hot milk and stir well. Reheat in the microwave for approximately 20 seconds to thoroughly heat, and stir well again for best taste. Make sure you share these with your neighbors since they are too cute to keep to yourself!

Melting Mummy Cocoa Bombs

These mummies are wrapped in white fondant "bandages" that have a little bit of blood seeping out. . . . Gross! These mummies are sure to equally delight and distress anyone who receives one, especially if you add red powder to the inside so it's obvious the mummy was still . . . fresh. Fondant creates a 3-D and realistic-looking bandage wrap for the mummies, and is easily found in the baking section of most larger grocery stores. Don't be intimidated by it; it's ready to use and eat, and is basically sugar play dough. It will harden rather quickly, though, so it's best to use these within the first 3 days of making them, or the fondant might not completely melt into the hot cocoa. If you don't have or want to buy fondant, feel free to simply use thick piped lines of white chocolate to create the bandages. I used red edible paint for the "blood" accents, but this is one case where regular food coloring (gel is best) will work just fine, since you're just decorating the exterior.

MAKES 6 REGULAR COCOA BOMBS

12 ounces bright white candy melts *or* white chocolate, tempered

1 recipe batch white cocoa mix (page 41) *or* ½ cup store-bought white cocoa

Red powdered food coloring, if desired

Gravestone sprinkle candies, if desired (*not* for young children)

½ cup dehydrated mini marshmallows

Extra melted white chocolate or edible glue

Edible monster eye decorations

6–8 ounces white prepared fondant

Red edible paint or food coloring

To Make: Place a hot cocoa bomb in the bottom of a mug. Add 10 ounces of very hot milk and stir well. Microwave for 20 extra seconds to thoroughly melt all ingredients for best taste. Let the hot milk unwrap your mummy . . . ahhhh!

Melt the chocolate thoroughly and pour 1–2 tablespoons melted chocolate into each mold and use a brush or the back of a spoon to make sure the chocolate fills in all of the mold and up the edges. Refrigerate 5 minutes to set. If the edges are thin, carefully brush more chocolate around the edges and refrigerate for 5 more minutes. Carefully unmold. Set aside 6 of the shells for the tops. Melt the edges of 6 of the shells that will be the bottoms. Fill these cocoa bomb shells with: 1 tablespoon white cocoa mix, a pinch of red powdered food coloring if desired, a gravestone or two, and a handful of dehydrated mini marshmallows. Melt the edges of the top half spheres and attach. Let set. To decorate, place a dot of melted white chocolate or edible glue on the back of each eye and attach two eyes to each mummy. Then create the fondant strips. Knead and soften the fondant, and roll it out to as thin as possible, about ⅛ inch. Cut into ¼-inch strips, and wrap around the cocoa bombs, adhering it to itself, or using a bit of melted chocolate or edible glue if needed. Use a brush or your fingers to add a bit of red food paint or coloring as if it were seeping out around the edges of the bandages. Repeat for all mummies.

Brain-Eating Zombie Cocoa Bombs

These zombie cocoa bombs are inspired by the un-dead or half-dead. Be they gray, green, or a mix of both, they're not something you want to encounter in real life! I used black oil-based food coloring to make these gray, and found sugar decorations of zombie hands to have breaking out of the cocoa bombs. Add sprinkles that represent zombie culture; I found bloody bones and brains, and gray brains, too. White cocoa mix is inside with a bit of black natural food coloring powder, which makes a lovely zombie-esque gray milk! The hands don't float, but boy do they look creepy when you lift one up with your spoon. (Or in this case, I used a butter knife for stirring, just in case I needed to defend myself. You know . . . hypothetically.)

MAKES 6 REGULAR COCOA BOMBS

12 ounces white candy melts colored gray *or* white chocolate, tempered and colored gray, divided
Black powdered food coloring
1 recipe batch white cocoa mix (page 41) *or* ½ cup store-bought white cocoa
Zombie-inspired sprinkles, such as bones and brains
Zombie hand decorations, if desired
2 ounces extra gray chocolate, melted, for decorating

To Make: Place a hot cocoa bomb in the bottom of a mug. Add 10 ounces of very hot milk and stir well. Get ready to defend yourself against the undead . . . or at least to have a zombie-gray tongue for awhile.

Melt the chocolate thoroughly and stir in the food coloring if necessary. Pour 1–2 tablespoons melted chocolate into each mold and use a brush or the back of a spoon to make sure the chocolate fills in all of the mold and up the edges. Refrigerate 5 minutes to set. If the edges are thin, carefully brush more chocolate around the edges and refrigerate for 5 more minutes. Carefully unmold. Set aside 6 of the shells for the tops. Melt the edges of 6 of the shells that will be the bottoms. Fill these cocoa bomb shells with: 1 tablespoon white cocoa mix, a handful of sprinkles, and a zombie hand if not using it on the exterior. Melt the edges of the leftover shells and attach the tops. Let set. To decorate, transfer the leftover gray chocolate to a piping bag or plastic bag and cut the tip. Pipe lines across both directions and add sprinkles. To attach zombie hands, dip the bottoms heavily in melted gray chocolate and hold lightly in place for 30 seconds. Then refrigerate 5 minutes until set. For the ones coming out of the sides, either break off part of the bottom shell before attached the two spheres, or use a knife to very carefully break off part below the seam. Insert the zombie hand dipped in gray chocolate and hold in place lightly for 30 seconds, then refrigerate for 5 minutes until set.

Frankenstein's Monster Cocoa Bombs

Dr. Frankenstein has been cooking up something creepy in the kitchen . . . a green cocoa bomb creature that comes alive when you add it to hot milk! Really, it's just a green cocoa bomb that explodes with marshmallows and lightning bolts. But it does turn your cocoa an eerie shade of green. Frankenstein's monster doesn't actually have a name, so feel free to name your cocoa bombs whatever you'd like. You could also easily create Frankenstein's monster's bride, if you were so inclined!

MAKES 6 REGULAR COCOA BOMBS

10–12 ounces green candy melts *or* **white chocolate, tempered and colored green**
1 recipe batch white cocoa mix (page 41) *or* **½ cup store-bought white cocoa**
½ cup mini marshmallows
Lightning bolt sprinkles
2 ounces melted very dark bar chocolate, 80% cocoa or higher, for decorating
Edible monster eyes, for decorating

Melt the chocolate thoroughly. Pour 1–2 tablespoons melted chocolate into each mold and use a brush or the back of a spoon to make sure the chocolate fills in all of the mold and up the edges. Refrigerate 5 minutes to set. If the edges are thin, carefully brush more chocolate around the edges and refrigerate for 5 more minutes. Carefully unmold. Set aside 6 of the shells for the tops. Melt the edges of 6 of the shells that will be the bottoms. Fill these cocoa bomb shells with: 1 tablespoon white cocoa mix, a handful of mini marshmallows, and a few lightning bolt sprinkles. Melt the edges of the leftover shells and attach the tops. Let set. To decorate, melt the dark chocolate just until melted enough to dip a brush into. Make sure it isn't too hot or scorched, or it will melt the green chocolate! Use the chocolate and the brush to create the hair, mouth, and scars as desired. Dab a bit of the melted chocolate to attach the edible eyes on top of each cocoa bomb. Let all dry thoroughly.

To Make: Place a hot cocoa bomb in the bottom of a mug. Add 10 ounces of very hot milk and stir well. Make sure to stay far, far away from lightning, just in case.

Salted Caramel Deluxe Cocoa Bombs

Whoever figured out that salt elevates caramel to the next level of flavor was a genius. My favorite salt to use are Maldon sea salt flakes, but you can also use crunchy sea salt if you prefer. Sea salt flakes melt beautifully, and are just fancy (and expensive). Look on the very bottom shelf in the spice aisle for Maldon sea salt flakes. If you use salted caramel candy melts, don't add extra salt to the chocolate. If you're working on your tempering skills, this is a great time to try tempering "gold" or "caramel" couverture chocolate, which will give you a lovely golden color. I love the swirl of golden deliciousness this simple cocoa bomb creates.

MAKES 6 REGULAR OR 10–12 MINI COCOA BOMBS

Gold luster dust or edible glitter
12 ounces caramel or salted caramel candy melts *or* white chocolate, tempered and colored caramel *or* gold/caramel couverture, tempered
¼–½ teaspoon caramel flavoring oil, *only* if using unflavored chocolate
½–1 teaspoon sea salt or salt flakes *only* if using unsalted chocolate
1 recipe batch white cocoa mix (page 41) *or* ½ cup store-bought mix

To Make: Place a hot cocoa bomb in the bottom of a mug. Add 10 ounces of very hot milk and stir well. Enjoy a shimmery, golden-sweet treat.

Use a dry, fluffy, food-only brush to coat half of the molds with gold luster or edible glitter powder. Melt the chocolate and thoroughly stir in the flavoring if necessary, to taste. If your chocolate is not already salted, add ½–1 teaspoon sea salt, to taste. Pour 1–2 tablespoons of the melted chocolate into each mold and use a brush or the back of a spoon to make sure the chocolate fills in all of the mold and up the edges. Refrigerate 5 minutes to set. If the edges are thin, carefully brush more chocolate around the edges and refrigerate for 5 more minutes. Carefully unmold. Set aside 6 of the shells for the tops. Melt the edges of 6 of the shells that will be the bottoms. Fill these cocoa bomb shells with 1 tablespoon white cocoa mix. Melt the edges of the leftover shells and attach the tops. Let set.

Peanut Butter Is for Lovers Cocoa Bombs

I only know one person in my life who does not like the combination of chocolate and peanut butter. I don't know what happened to their taste buds, but hopefully they'll grow to like it! If anything is going to change their mind, this hot cocoa bomb might do the trick. Have you tried peanut butter powder? It's right in the peanut butter aisle, and great to have on hand for all sorts of things, particularly for adding to smoothies or oatmeal. It's only slightly more expensive than a jar of regular peanut butter, so throw one in your cart next time you're shopping so you can make this delectable hot cocoa bomb. It becomes thick, rich, creamy, and oh-so-satisfying. This can easily become too rich, so feel free to tone down the recipe a bit by skipping the cocoa mix or toppings, or adding more milk. These also make fantastic mini cocoa bombs for a small, rich serving of cocoa. Simply use the below recipe to make 10–12 mini (2-inch) bombs and place 1 tablespoon of cocoa mix inside each.

MAKES 6 REGULAR OR 10–12 MINI COCOA BOMBS

12 ounces milk chocolate candy melts *or* milk chocolate, tempered
1 recipe batch hot cocoa mix (page 40) *or* ½ cup store-bought mix
6 tablespoons peanut butter powder
½ teaspoon salt
Mini peanut butter cookies plus extra for decorating
Mini dehydrated marshmallows
Mini chocolate-peanut-butter cups, plus extra for decorating
½ cup peanut butter, for decorating, optional
1 cup sifted powdered sugar for decorating, optional

Melt the chocolate and thoroughly stir in the flavoring. Pour 1–2 tablespoons melted chocolate into each mold and use a brush or the back of a spoon to make sure the chocolate fills in all of the mold and up the edges. Refrigerate 5 minutes to set. If the edges are thin, carefully brush more chocolate around the edges and refrigerate for 5 more minutes. Carefully unmold. Set aside 6 of the shells for the tops. Melt the edges of 6 of the shells that will be the bottoms. Fill these cocoa bomb shells with: 1 tablespoon hot cocoa mix, 1 tablespoon peanut butter powder, and a few grains of salt. Add mini cookies and mini marshmallows to each of the bottom shells as well, if desired. Melt the edges of the leftover shells and attach the tops. Let set. To decorate, place the ½ cup of peanut butter in a microwave-safe bowl and microwave for 30 seconds, until slightly melted. Mix the sifted powdered sugar in until the peanut butter is a good texture for piping. You may not need all of it. Transfer to a piping bag or plastic bag, snip the corner, and pipe peanut butter lines back and forth across the finished bombs. Attach a few cookies or peanut butter cups to the top of each bomb while the peanut butter is still soft.

To Make: Place a hot cocoa bomb in the bottom of a mug. Add 10 ounces of very hot milk and stir well. Reheat in the microwave for approximately 20 seconds to thoroughly heat, and stir well again for best taste. Best enjoyed while wearing a flannel and sitting out on the porch when there's a chill in the air.

Chocolate-Peanut Butter-Pretzel Cocoa Bombs

This is a classic fall flavor combination that just evokes memories of crisp nights at football games or the drive-in movie theatre. I made these as hearts because I love this combination so much, but feel free to use whatever shape you'd like. Adding a bit of extra sea salt inside the cocoa bomb evokes that pretzel flavor. The peanut butter powder creates a thick, luscious peanut-buttery cocoa, so feel free to add a bit less peanut butter powder or a bit more milk if you prefer it thinner.

MAKES APPROX. 8 HEART COCOA BOMBS

- **12 ounces white candy melts *or* white chocolate, tempered and colored tan**
- **1 recipe batch hot cocoa mix (page 40) *or* ½ cup store-bought mix**
- **6 tablespoons peanut butter powder**
- **½ teaspoon sea salt or salt flakes**
- **½ cup crushed pretzels, plus extra for decorating**
- **½ cup mini dehydrated marshmallows, if desired**
- **2 ounces milk or dark chocolate, for decorating**

Melt the chocolate and pour 1–2 tablespoons into each mold and use a brush or the back of a spoon to make sure the chocolate fills in all of the mold and up the edges. Refrigerate 5 minutes to set. If the edges are thin, carefully brush more chocolate around the edges and refrigerate for 5 more minutes. Carefully unmold. Set aside 6 of the shells for the tops. Melt the edges of 6 of the shells that will be the bottoms. Fill these cocoa bomb shells with: 1 tablespoon hot cocoa mix, 1 tablespoon peanut butter powder, and a few grains of salt. Add a handful of crushed pretzels and mini marshmallows to each of the bottom shells as well, if desired. Melt the edges of the leftover shells and attach the tops. Let set. To decorate, melt the 2 ounces of extra chocolate. Transfer to a piping bag or plastic bag, snip the corner, and pipe peanut butter lines back and forth across the finished bombs. Attach some crushed pretzels to each bomb.

To Make: Place a hot cocoa bomb in the bottom of a mug. Add 10 ounces very hot milk and stir well. Reheat in the microwave for approximately 20 seconds to thoroughly heat, and stir well again for best taste. Root for your favorite football team, be it on the big screen or on the local school field.

Chocolate-Ginger Cocoa Bombs

Chocolate and ginger are a classic flavor combination, and the warmth of the combination is perfect as the weather starts to take a turn for cold. Speaking of which, if you are on the tail end of a cold, this drink is so warming and opens the sinuses with that strong ginger kick. Of course it also warms and settles the belly, which colds can sometimes get into a bit of a bother. These are also delicious made with a dark chocolate shell and a dark cocoa mix, if you prefer a stronger flavor profile.

MAKES 6 REGULAR COCOA BOMBS

12 ounces milk chocolate candy melts *or* **milk chocolate, tempered**
¼–½ teaspoon ginger flavoring oil *or* **1 teaspoon dried ginger powder**
1 recipe batch hot cocoa mix (page 40) *or* **½ cup store-bought mix**
Chopped dried candied ginger, plus extra for decorating
Gold shimmer pearl sprinkles, plus extra for decorating
Dried ginger powder, for decorating
Edible glue or extra melted chocolate, for decorating

Melt the chocolate and add either the flavoring oil or powder. Pour 1–2 tablespoons melted chocolate into each mold and use a brush or the back of a spoon to make sure the chocolate fills in all of the mold and up the edges. Refrigerate 5 minutes to set. If the edges are thin, carefully brush more chocolate around the edges and refrigerate for 5 more minutes. Carefully unmold. Set aside 6 of the shells for the tops. Melt the edges of 6 of the shells that will be the bottoms. Fill these cocoa bomb shells with: 1 tablespoon hot cocoa mix, a dash of ginger powder, a piece or a few of candied ginger, and a few gold shimmer pearl sprinkles. Melt the edges of the leftover shells and attach the tops. Let set. To decorate, either heat the top of the cocoa bomb with a crème brûlée torch or add a thin coating of edible glue or melted chocolate. Attach a beautiful piece of candied ginger and a few extra gold shimmer pearls. Repeat for all cocoa bombs.

To Make: Place a hot cocoa bomb in the bottom of a mug. Add 10 ounces of very hot milk and stir well. Send that gingery warmth to the tips of your toes and the ends of your fingers and feel rejuvenated.

Snowball Cocoa Bombs

Snowmen belong outside, not in a hot milk bath where they . . . gasp . . . melt! But a snowball, glistening with silver snowflakes and silver foil on top, is perfectly suited for melting into a delicious cocoa. If you do want to make a snowman, it's easy to transform a snowball into one, and it's especially cute if you add carrot sprinkles, round black edible dragées (coal), and mitten sprinkles. It's up to you to decide if you think snowballs taste like peppermint or vanilla, as both are delicious. In fact, I like the combination, too!

MAKES 6 REGULAR COCOA BOMBS

12 ounces bright white candy melts
   ***or* white chocolate, tempered**
⅛–¼ teaspoon peppermint *or*
   1 teaspoon vanilla flavoring oil,
   to taste, optional
1 recipe batch white cocoa mix
   (page 41) *or* ½ cup store-bought
   mix
Snowflake sprinkles
1 cup dehydrated mini
   marshmallows, divided
Edible glue, extra white chocolate,
   coconut or vegetable oil, or
   shortening, for decorating
Edible silver glitter
Edible silver foil for decorating,
   optional

To Make: Place a hot cocoa bomb in the bottom of a mug. Add 10 ounces of very hot milk and stir well. Breathe a sigh of relief that your cocoa bomb was a random snowball, and not part of a snowman.

Melt the chocolate and thoroughly stir in the flavoring oil to taste. Pour 1–2 tablespoons of the melted chocolate into each mold and use a brush or the back of a spoon to make sure the chocolate fills in all of the mold and up the edges. Refrigerate 5 minutes to set. If the edges are thin, carefully brush more chocolate around the edges and refrigerate for 5 more minutes. Carefully unmold. Set aside 6 of the shells for the tops. Melt the edges of 6 of the shells that will be the bottoms. Fill these cocoa bomb shells with: 1 tablespoon white cocoa mix, a few snowflake sprinkles, and a handful of dehydrated mini marshmallows (don't use more than ½ cup altogether). Melt the edges of the leftover shells and attach the tops. Let set. To decorate, begin by putting the remaining ½ cup dehydrated mini marshmallows in a plastic bag and crushing them by using the back of a rolling pin or wooden spoon until they are powdered and mostly fine. Use a brush to cover the tops (or entirely—it's up to you!) of each ball with a thin coating of edible glue, chocolate, coconut or vegetable oil, or shortening. Then roll each top or entire bomb in the crushed mini marshmallows to create the effect of a snowball. Sprinkle the top with a tiny bit of silver glitter to make it glimmer, and add a few snowflake sprinkles if desired. Use a brush or food-only tweezers to add a small piece of edible silver foil to the top of each bomb.

Candy Cane Cocoa Bombs

Candy canes are a classic addition to regular hot cocoa, but I think the peppermint flavor pairs even better with white hot cocoa. Feel free to make this in a milk or dark chocolate shell with regular hot cocoa mix, too. This is a fun party drink or party favor. Miniature candy cane sprinkles are the perfect festive touch as they come floating to the top. Peppermint flavoring oil (not extract!) is extremely strong, so be sure to start with less and taste as you add. Around the holidays you can often find candy canes shaped like spoons, which are specifically made for stirring hot cocoa or coffee. They make a fun addition if you're gifting these cocoa bombs.

MAKES 6 REGULAR COCOA BOMBS

12 ounces bright white candy melts *or* white chocolate, tempered

⅛–¼ teaspoon peppermint flavoring oil, to taste

1 recipe batch white cocoa mix (page 41) *or* ½ cup store-bought mix

Mini candy cane sprinkles

Peppermint marshmallows

Candy cane shaped cake toppers, optional

½ cup dehydrated mini marshmallows

¼ cup crushed candy canes, optional

2 ounces red candy melts *or* white chocolate, tempered and colored red, for decorating

Extra candy cane sprinkles, crushed candy canes, and/or candy cane toppers, for decorating

If desired, add a sprinkle of the mini candy cane sprinkles to the bottom of a few of the molds. Melt the chocolate and thoroughly stir in the flavoring oil to taste. Pour 1–2 tablespoons melted chocolate into each mold and use a brush or the back of a spoon to make sure the chocolate fills in all of the mold and up the edges. Refrigerate 5 minutes to set. If the edges are thin, carefully brush more chocolate around the edges and refrigerate for 5 more minutes. Carefully unmold. Set aside 6 of the shells for the tops. Melt the edges of 6 of the shells that will be the bottoms. Fill these cocoa bomb shells with: 1 tablespoon white cocoa mix, a good sprinkle of candy cane sprinkles, a peppermint marshmallow, a candy cane shaped candy topper, and a handful of dehydrated mini marshmallows. Melt the edges of the leftover shells and attach the tops. Let set. Melt the 2 ounces of white chocolate and add to a piping bag or plastic bag. Snip a tiny part of the corner and pipe lines across the cocoa bombs. Sprinkle with a small amount of candy cane sprinkles, crushed candy canes, and/ or a candy cane topper.

To Make: Place a hot cocoa bomb in the bottom of a mug. Add 10 ounces of very hot milk and stir well. This is a fun one to pour into a thermos and bring with you while you drive around town to look at Christmas lights!

Black Forest Cake in a Cup Cocoa Bombs

Black forest cake is a decadent chocolate-cherry-cream cake that evokes the Black Forest in Germany and it's deep, enchanting flavors. The cake is usually beautifully decorated with chocolate curls, cocoa, whipped cream swirls, cherries, and sometimes powdered sugar snow. A traditional black forest cake can be so intricately decorated it looks like a cuckoo clock from the same region became edible! To imitate that feeling, I've added mini meringues dipped in chocolate and freeze-dried tart cherries to the cocoa bomb. The cherries in black forest cake are usually sour cherries to counteract the otherworldly sweetness, and traditionally kirsch is added as well. Feel free to add a dash of kirsch to your cup of cocoa if you'd like!

MAKES 6 REGULAR COCOA BOMBS

10 ounces dark chocolate candy melts *or* tempered dark chocolate

½–1 teaspoon washington, black, or tart cherry flavoring oil, to taste

1 recipe batch hot cocoa mix (page 40) *or* ½ cup store-bought mix

½ cup dehydrated mini marshmallows

Vanilla mini meringues, chocolate-covered or plain, optional

Freeze-dried tart cherries

A small amount of melted chocolate *or* edible glue, for decorating

Melt the chocolate and thoroughly stir in the flavoring oil to taste. Pour 1–2 tablespoons melted chocolate into each mold and use a brush or the back of a spoon to make sure the chocolate fills in all of the mold and up the edges. Refrigerate 5 minutes to set. If the edges are thin, carefully brush more chocolate around the edges and refrigerate for 5 more minutes. Carefully unmold. Set aside 6 of the shells for the tops. Melt the edges of 6 of the shells that will be the bottoms. Fill these cocoa bomb shells with: 1 tablespoon hot cocoa mix, a handful of dehydrated mini marshmallows, a mini meringue, and a few freeze-dried tart cherries. Melt the edges of the leftover shells and attach the tops. Let set. Use a dab of melted chocolate or edible glue to attach a mini meringue to the top of each cocoa bomb.

To Make: Place a hot cocoa bomb in the bottom of a mug. Add 10 ounces of very hot milk and stir well. Reheat in the microwave for approximately 20 seconds to thoroughly heat, and stir well again for best taste. I definitely recommend adding plenty of real whipped cream on top and a bit of kirsch if you'd like!

Bûche de Noël Cocoa Bombs

If you're not sure what in the world this cocoa bomb is called, how to pronounce it, or what it is supposed to be flavored like, you've been missing out on a traditional European Christmas-season cake called "Bûche de Noël." In its namesake French, this translates as "The Christmas Log" cake. A jelly roll-style chocolate cake filled with cream filling, the cake is shaped and decorated like a log, complete with chocolate shards for bark, powdered sugar for snow, and meringue mushrooms. This classic cake is crafted after the actual Christmas log, thrown on the fire for good luck and to keep the family warm on Christmas. This hot cocoa bomb is reminiscent of that delightful cake and all of its old-fashioned charm. The milk chocolate shell has Bavarian cream flavoring added. There is no powder inside this bomb; instead, a healthy scoop of hazelnut spread brings another European-favorite flavor. Of course these are decorated with the traditional toppers: chocolate "bark," powdered-sugar snow, and mushroom cookies! The taste is worthy of celebration indeed.

MAKES 6 REGULAR COCOA BOMBS

12 ounces milk chocolate candy melts *or* tempered milk chocolate

½–1 teaspoon Bavarian cream flavoring oil, to taste

1 recipe batch hot cocoa mix (page 40) *or* ½ cup store-bought mix

½ cup milk chocolate candy melts *or* tempered milk chocolate

1 cup hazelnut spread

2 tablespoons cinnamon

18 mushroom cookies, optional

Powdered sugar for decorating, optional

Edible glue or extra melted chocolate for decorating, optional

Melt the chocolate and thoroughly stir in the flavoring oils to taste. Pour 1–2 tablespoons melted chocolate into each mold and use a brush or the back of a spoon to make sure the chocolate fills in all of the mold and up the edges. Refrigerate 5 minutes to set. If the edges are thin, carefully brush more chocolate around the edges and refrigerate for 5 more minutes. Carefully unmold. Set aside 6 of the shells for the tops. Melt the edges of 6 of the shells that will be the bottoms. Fill these cocoa bomb shells with: 1 tablespoon hazelnut spread, ¼ teaspoon cinnamon, and a few mushroom cookies. Melt the edges of the leftover shells and attach the tops. Let set. Meanwhile, melt ½ cup chocolate wafers carefully in 10-second intervals, until thoroughly melted. Spread out on a sheet of parchment or wax paper as thinly as possible while not being able to see through it. Place in the refrigerator for a few minutes. To decorate, break the flat chocolate into shards. Use a brush with a bit of melted chocolate or a dab of edible glue to attach shards of chocolate to the shell, as well as a mushroom cookie. Repeat for all cocoa bombs. Dust lightly with powdered sugar.

To Make: Place a hot cocoa bomb in the bottom of a mug. Add 10 ounces of very hot milk and stir well. Reheat in the microwave for approximately 20 seconds to thoroughly heat, and stir well again for best taste. Sit by the fireplace (or play that fake fireplace on the television!) and stare out the window longingly, remembering Christmases past and enjoying the thought of Christmases future.

Chocolate Cherry Cocoa Bombs

Chocolate and cherry is a classic winter flavor combination, especially when added to a hot cocoa mix that creates a luxurious specialty cocoa. These look particularly attractive topped with a glitter-dipped cherry that looks like art! (To be totally honest, I couldn't find fresh cherries in March, so I used fake ones in these photos, but real ones will be even more fantastic if you can find them.) This is also delicious made with dark chocolate cocoa bomb shells and a dark specialty cocoa mix. If your family is anything like mine, Grandma probably likes those cherry cordial candies, so chances are she will love this cocoa, too.

MAKES 6 REGULAR COCOA BOMBS

12 ounces milk chocolate candy melts *or* milk chocolate, tempered
½ teaspoon Washington or black cherry flavoring oil, to taste
1 recipe batch hot cocoa mix (page 40) *or* ½ cup store-bought mix
½ cup mini dehydrated marshmallows
Red edible glitter, plus extra for decorating
Freeze-dried cherries
6 real, washed and thoroughly dried cherries with stems
Edible glue or extra melted chocolate

Melt the chocolate and thoroughly stir in the flavoring oil to taste. Pour 1–2 tablespoons melted chocolate into each mold and use a brush or the back of a spoon to make sure the chocolate fills in all of the mold and up the edges. Refrigerate 5 minutes to set. If the edges are thin, carefully brush more chocolate around the edges and refrigerate for 5 more minutes. Carefully unmold. Set aside 6 of the shells for the tops. Melt the edges of 6 of the shells that will be the bottoms. Fill these cocoa bomb shells with: 1 tablespoon hot cocoa mix, plenty of mini marshmallows, a sprinkle of red edible glitter, and a few freeze-dried cherries. Melt the edges of the leftover shells and attach the tops. Let set. Dip the cherries in edible glitter, and attach by either using a bit of edible glue or extra melted chocolate. Steady them until they are lightly set, then refrigerate for 10 minutes to fully set.

To Make: Place a hot cocoa bomb in the bottom of a mug. Add 8–10 ounces of very hot milk and stir well. Microwave for an additional 20 seconds and stir well again to create the best taste. Don't forget to add a cherry cordial to Grandma's cup!

Chocolate Peppermint Cocoa Bombs

This flavor combination always reminds me of my January birthday, when I used to always request a crème de menthe cake with chocolate frosting. If your mind immediately went to the alcohol, think instead of the thick green syrup usually found at soda fountains and put on sundaes or in milkshakes. The syrup is hard to find (if you do find it, it's usually in a small glass bottle by the ice cream toppings), so some years I had to do without. Other years, I was able to track some down by going to a local diner and asking them to pump enough of the syrup in a cup for me to make the cake. They politely obliged the crazy girl asking for a cup full of thick, sweet mint syrup. Thankfully, the flavor is now much easier to achieve with crème de menthe flavoring oil, which, added to the chocolate, creates a delightfully cool, creamy, peppermint flavor.

MAKES 6 REGULAR COCOA BOMBS

12 ounces dark chocolate candy melts *or* **dark chocolate, tempered**

¼–½ teaspoon crème de menthe flavoring oil or peppermint oil, to taste

1 recipe batch hot cocoa mix (page 40) *or* **½ cup store-bought mix**

½ cup mini dehydrated marshmallows

Mini mint cream-filled chocolate candies

Red and green sprinkles, such as trees and ornaments or holly and berries

2 ounces green candy melts *or* **white chocolate, tempered and colored green**

Red, green, and white nonpareils, for decorating

Melt the chocolate and thoroughly stir in the flavoring oil to taste. Pour 1–2 tablespoons melted chocolate into each mold and use a brush or the back of a spoon to make sure the chocolate fills in all of the mold and up the edges. Refrigerate 5 minutes to set. If the edges are thin, carefully brush more chocolate around the edges and refrigerate for 5 more minutes. Carefully unmold. Set aside 6 of the shells for the tops. Melt the edges of 6 of the shells that will be the bottoms. Fill these cocoa bomb shells with: 1 tablespoon hot cocoa mix and plenty of mini marshmallows. Add a few mini mint cream–filled chocolate candies and a handful of sprinkles. Melt the edges of the leftover shells and attach the tops. Let set. Melt the 2 ounces of green chocolate and add to a piping bag or plastic bag. Snip a tiny part of the corner and pipe thin lines across the cocoa bombs. Decorate with nonpareils.

> **To Make:** Place a hot cocoa bomb in the bottom of a mug. Add 8 –10 ounces of very hot milk and stir well. Scheme of where you can find crème de menthe syrup to make a crème de menthe cake with chocolate frosting . . .

Vanilla Noel Cocoa Bombs

This is the vanilla lover's dream hot cocoa. White hot cocoa can often be bland and much more on the milky side than the vanilla side. But have no fear! I've added vanilla, vanilla, and vanilla for this recipe! It absolutely envelops you in voluptuous vanilla-ness. Just make sure you don't use your standard baking vanilla extract here, as that will ruin your chocolate. You'll need an oil-based vanilla flavoring, which can easily be found in most candy- and cake-making aisles of major stores. Then you'll add ground vanilla beans to the white chocolate exterior for those perfect flecks of "French vanilla." White vanilla powder sweetens up the cocoa mix inside and completes the vanilla trio. Vanilla powder may be ordered from plenty of specialty purveyors, but I'm particularly fond of Nielsen-Massey vanilla powder or Cook's vanilla powder. Both have an old-fashioned styling that makes me swoon, plus they taste great. A bit spendy perhaps, but you get what you pay for when it comes to vanilla. A moment of vanilla bliss will be worth it.

MAKES 6 REGULAR COCOA BOMBS

Silver luster powder or edible glitter

12 ounces white candy melts *or* white chocolate, tempered

1 teaspoon vanilla flavoring oil, or to taste

1 teaspoon ground vanilla beans/ vanilla bean powder

1 recipe batch white cocoa mix (page 41) *or* ½ cup store-bought mix

2 tablespoons (6 teaspoons) vanilla powder

½ cup mini dehydrated marshmallows

A tiny amount of melted white chocolate *or* edible glue, for decorating

White shimmer sprinkles, for decorating

Use a large dry, food-only brush to coat 6 of the molds with silver luster powder or edible glitter. Melt the chocolate and thoroughly stir in the flavoring oil to taste and the 1 teaspoon of ground vanilla beans. Pour 1–2 tablespoons of the melted chocolate into each mold and use a brush or the back of a spoon to make sure the chocolate fills in all of the mold and up the edges. Refrigerate 5 minutes to set. If the edges are thin, carefully brush more chocolate around the edges and refrigerate for 5 more minutes. Carefully unmold. Set aside 6 of the shells for the tops. Melt the edges of 6 of the shells that will be the bottoms. Fill these cocoa bomb shells with: 1 tablespoon white hot cocoa mix and 1 teaspoon vanilla powder in each. Add plenty of mini marshmallows to each of the bottom shells as well. Melt the edges of the leftover shells and attach the tops. Let set. If the shells need a touch-up, dust them with extra silver luster powder. Place a small dab of white chocolate or edible glue on top and sprinkle with a few shimmery white sprinkles.

To Make: Place a hot cocoa bomb in the bottom of a mug. Add 10 ounces of very hot milk and stir well. If anyone tries to tell you vanilla is boring or bland, just keep letting them think that and keep all of these cocoa bombs to yourself.

Spiked Eggnog Cocoa Bombs

These beautiful cocoa bombs can be naughty or nice. They're creamy and spicy served as is, or a little bit naughty served spiked with some rum or cognac. The classic spices of eggnog and Bavarian cream flavoring oil added to the white chocolate combine to emulate the true flavor of eggnog. These make fantastic gifts at the holidays placed in sturdy fluted cupcake liners wrapped in cellophane and tied with ribbons. Add a vintage spoon or some Christmas-themed straws to complete the gift.

MAKES 6 REGULAR COCOA BOMBS

1 teaspoon cinnamon
½ teaspoon nutmeg
¼ teaspoon allspice *or* ground cloves
½ ounces white candy melts *or* white chocolate, tempered
½ teaspoon Bavarian cream flavoring oil, to taste
1 recipe batch white cocoa mix (page 41) *or* ½ cup store-bought mix
½ cup mini dehydrated marshmallows

Mix the cinnamon, nutmeg, and allspice or cloves in a small bowl. Use a large dry, food-only brush to coat 6 of the molds with the spice mix. Most of it will go to the center; that's fine. Melt the chocolate and thoroughly stir in the flavoring oil to taste. Pour 1–2 tablespoons melted chocolate into each mold and use a brush or the back of a spoon to make sure the chocolate fills in all of the mold and up the edges. Refrigerate 5 minutes to set. If the edges are thin, carefully brush more chocolate around the edges and refrigerate for 5 more minutes. Carefully unmold. Set aside 6 of the shells for the tops. Melt the edges of 6 of the shells that will be the bottoms. Fill these cocoa bomb shells with: 1 tablespoon white hot cocoa mix and a handful of mini marshmallows. Melt the edges of the leftover shells and attach the tops. Let set.

To Make: Place a hot cocoa bomb in the bottom of a mug. Add 8–10 ounces of very hot milk and stir well. Serve with a splash of rum, if desired. Light the tree, play some Christmas music, wrap the presents, light the candles . . . this eggnog is sure to get you in the holiday mood!

Gingerbread Cocoa Bombs

There are two ways to make this fun recipe: regular cocoa bombs or gingerbread men! If you do use a gingerbread man mold, the back will be open, displaying the cocoa mix and mini marshmallows that have stuck into the chocolate. Either way, this recipe brings all the deliciousness of dunking a gingerbread man cookie into a cup of hot cocoa. They make a perfect holiday gift!

MAKES 6 REGULAR COCOA BOMBS
*OPTIONAL: GINGERBREAD MAN MOLD WILL MAKE 6–8

12 ounces white candy melts *or* white chocolate, tempered and colored brown *or* 12 ounces milk chocolate candy melts *or* milk chocolate, tempered
1 teaspoon gingerbread flavoring oil, to taste *or* 1 teaspoon ground ginger powder
1 recipe batch hot cocoa mix (page 40) *or* ½ cup store-bought mix
Additional ground ginger powder
½ cup mini dehydrated marshmallows
2 ounces milk chocolate candy wafers *or* milk chocolate, tempered
Gingerbread cookie shaped sprinkles

To Make: Place a hot cocoa bomb in the bottom of a mug. Add 8–10 ounces of very hot milk and stir well. Add whipped cream and sprinkle with ginger powder, cocoa powder, and gingerbread sprinkles for the full effect.

To make round bombs: Melt the chocolate and thoroughly stir in the flavoring oil or powder to taste. Pour 1–2 tablespoons of the melted chocolate into each mold and use a brush or the back of a spoon to make sure the chocolate fills in all of the mold and up the edges. Refrigerate 5 minutes to set. If the edges are thin, carefully brush more chocolate around the edges and refrigerate for 5 more minutes. Carefully unmold. Set aside 6 of the shells for the tops. Melt the edges of 6 of the shells that will be the bottoms. Fill these cocoa bomb shells with: 1 tablespoon hot cocoa mix, a dash of ginger powder, and a handful of mini marshmallows. Melt the edges of the leftover shells and attach the tops. Let set. Melt the extra 2 ounces of chocolate and add to a piping bag. Snip off a very small amount of the piping bag tip and pipe lines across the bombs. Sprinkle with gingerbread shaped sprinkles.

To make shaped bombs: Fill the gingerbread mold halfway full with chocolate. Add the tablespoon of hot cocoa mix and a few mini marshmallows and push them into the chocolate with the back of a spoon. Shake and tap the mold to settle everything into the chocolate. Refrigerate for 10–15 minutes or until solid. Very carefully remove from mold.

New Year's Eve Cocoa Countdown Balls

When I found a tiny crate of miniature bottles of champagne chocolate, filled with a champagne-flavored liqueur, I just had to make a New Year's Eve Countdown ball! These are a fun cocoa bomb to serve with a small wooden mallet and smash before adding to your mug, because then you can grab the chocolate bottle if you want before it starts to melt. I've also added shimmering metallic dragées and a "firework" of gold glitter on top. Your New Year's Eve guests are sure to love this drink almost as much as a glass of champagne to toast the new year!

MAKES 6 REGULAR COCOA BOMBS

10–12 ounces dark chocolate candy melts *or* dark chocolate, tempered
1 recipe batch white cocoa mix (page 41) *or* ½ cup store-bought mix
Metallic multi-color edible dragées
½ cup mini dehydrated marshmallows
6 miniature chocolate bottles of champagne, plus extra for decorating
Edible gold glitter

Melt the chocolate and pour 1–2 tablespoons melted chocolate into each mold. Use a brush or the back of a spoon to make sure the chocolate fills in all of the mold and up the edges. Refrigerate 5 minutes to set. If the edges are thin, carefully brush more chocolate around the edges and refrigerate for 5 more minutes. Carefully unmold. Set aside 6 of the shells for the tops. Melt the edges of 6 of the shells that will be the bottoms. Fill these cocoa bomb shells with: 1 tablespoon white hot cocoa mix, a sprinkle of metallic dragées, and a handful of mini marshmallows. Add one unwrapped bottle of champagne chocolate, adding a dash of gold glitter to the center where the label would be, if desired. Melt the edges of the leftover shells and attach the tops. Let set. Decorate by splashing a good amount of gold glitter on top to create a firework effect.

> **To Make:** Place a hot cocoa bomb in the bottom of a mug. Add 10 ounces of very hot milk and stir well. Toast to the new year!

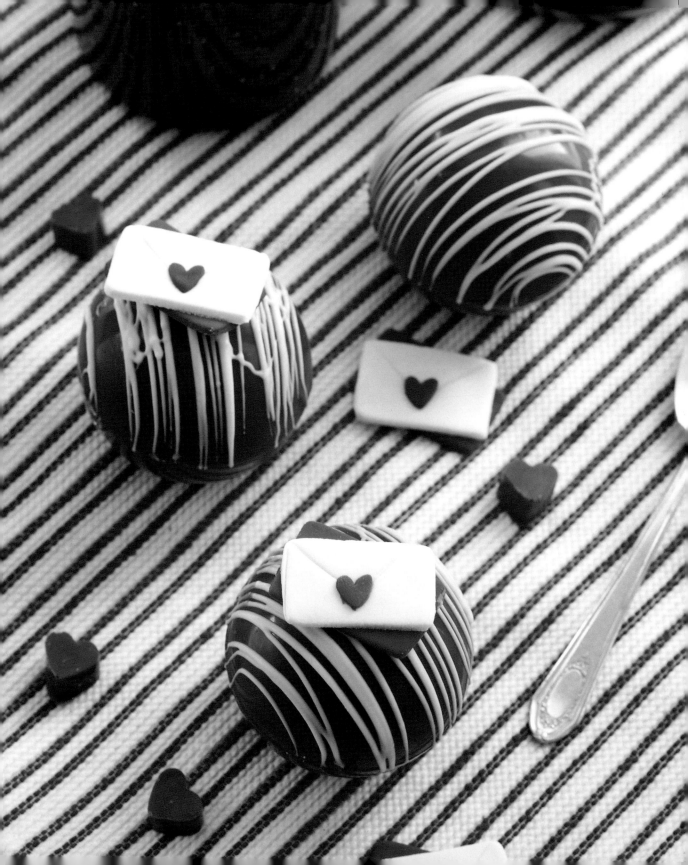

Red Velvet Romance Cocoa Bombs

Red velvet cake is a flavor that's hard to put your finger on, but you know it when you taste it, and you love it. That's why this red velvet cocoa bomb is all about the love! The classic red velvet cake is a southern favorite: cocoa-based cake with red coloring and cream cheese frosting. Red velvet flavoring oil adds all the right notes to this cocoa bomb, and it tastes like melting into a summer afternoon in the South on a big wrap-around porch with a big old slice of cake. It's enough to make you fall in love, so gift and serve this cocoa bomb with care. For extra fun, I spread the leftover red chocolate (if you have any left) into a very small (½ inch) silicone heart mold, refrigerated them, and popped them out. The decorations on top are made of fondant and attached with edible glue. You could also make this cocoa bomb with a dark chocolate shell and red velvet flavoring oil, then add red powdered food coloring to white cocoa mix inside to turn the drink red as a surprise.

MAKES 6 REGULAR COCOA BOMBS

12 ounces red candy melts *or* tempered white chocolate with red food coloring oil

½–1 teaspoon red velvet flavoring oil, or to taste

1 recipe batch white cocoa mix (page 41) *or* ½ cup store-bought mix

6 red chocolate hearts, optional

½ cup mini dehydrated marshmallows

2 ounces white chocolate candy melts *or* white chocolate, tempered, for decorating

Fondant love letter decorations, optional

Extra melted chocolate or edible glue for decorating

Melt the chocolate and thoroughly stir in the flavoring to taste. Pour 1–2 tablespoons melted chocolate into each mold and use a brush or the back of a spoon to make sure the chocolate fills in all of the mold and up the edges. Refrigerate 5 minutes to set. Carefully unmold. Set aside 6 of the shells for the tops. Melt the edges of 6 of the shells that will be the bottoms. Fill these cocoa bomb shells with 1 tablespoon white hot cocoa mix. Add one red heart and plenty of mini marshmallows to each of the bottom shells as well. Melt the edges of the leftover shells and attach the tops. Let set. Melt the 2 ounces of white chocolate and add to a piping bag or plastic bag. Snip a tiny part of the corner and pipe lines across the cocoa bombs. Decorate by using edible glue or melted chocolate to attach a secret love letter to the top of each cocoa bomb.

To Make: Place a hot cocoa bomb in the bottom of a mug. Add 10 ounces of very hot milk and stir well. Drink in the sweet nothings this cocoa will whisper to you.

Pretty in Pink Prosecco Cocoa Bombs

Shimmering pink prosecco has my name all over it. Add in plenty of white chocolate and this might be one of my surprise favorites in the book. It tastes like grown-up bubble gum and is a truly fun experience to drink. I recommend pairing it with some lovely self-care, such as a fluffy pink bathrobe and fuzzy slippers, a face mask, spa headband, fresh manicure, and the television all to yourself. If you can find Butler's pink champagne truffles to tuck inside, you won't regret spending a bit more on them. The box is so pretty, too! Any prosecco or champagne truffle that has white chocolate instead of milk or dark will work. You can also add other prosecco-flavored goodies, such as gummy bears, jelly bean bubbles, or jelly-filled bubble candies, as long as you're careful not to choke on them.

MAKES 6 REGULAR COCOA BOMBS

Rose gold or light pink luster dust
12 ounces pink candy melts *or* tempered white chocolate with pink food coloring oil
½ teaspoon sparkling wine flavoring oil, or to taste
1 recipe batch white cocoa mix (page 41) *or* ½ cup store-bought mix
½ teaspoon salt
6 pink champagne/prosecco white chocolate truffles
½ cup mini dehydrated marshmallows
A bit of melted white chocolate or edible glue, for decorating
Rose gold metallic flakes, for decorating

Use a clean, dry, fluffy brush to coat 12 half-sphere molds with the rose gold luster powder. Melt the chocolate and thoroughly stir in the flavoring to taste. Pour 1–2 tablespoons melted chocolate into each mold and use a brush or the back of a spoon to make sure the chocolate fills in all of the mold and up the edges. Refrigerate 5 minutes to set. Carefully unmold. Set aside 6 of the shells for the tops. Melt the edges of 6 of the shells that will be the bottoms. Fill these cocoa bomb shells with: 1 tablespoon white hot cocoa mix and a few grains of salt. Add one pink champagne truffle, plenty of mini marshmallows, and any desired sprinkles to each of the bottom shells as well. Melt the edges of the leftover shells and attach the tops. Let set. To decorate, place a tiny dab of melted chocolate or edible glue on the top of each cocoa bomb. Sprinkle the rose gold metallic flakes on top.

To Make: Place a hot cocoa bomb in the bottom of a mug. Add 10 ounces of very hot milk and stir well. Sit in front of the television with your feet up and think of nothing but the pink deliciousness you're drinking. Maybe grab an extra truffle or two. Ahhhh, bliss.

Ladies Who Brunch Mimosa Cocoa Bombs

These are the bombs you give your best gal pals when they've had a rough day, or when you have a winter "Let's Wear Real Clothes" weekend girls night (or a "Wear Pajamas" one). This cocoa bomb is judgment-free, heart-shaped, and will give you the warm fuzzies without the actual alcohol (unless you sneak a little in; no judgement, remember?). They also make fun bridal shower or engagement party favors, dressed up in fancy gold boxes or gold cupcake liners in a clear bag.

MAKES 6 HEART HOT COCOA BOMBS

12 ounces white candy melts *or* **tempered white chocolate, ready to use**
½ teaspoon sparkling wine flavoring oil, or to taste
¼ teaspoon orange flavoring oil, or to taste
1 recipe batch white cocoa mix (page 41) *or* **½ cup store-bought mix**
½ cup mini dehydrated marshmallows
2 ounces orange candy melts plus 1 ounce white candy melts, or 3 ounces white chocolate, tempered and colored light orange, for decorating
2 ounces white candy melts *or* **white chocolate, tempered, for decorating**
Gold and white sugar pearls, for decorating

Melt the chocolate and thoroughly stir in both flavoring oils to taste. Pour 1–2 tablespoons melted chocolate into each mold and use a brush or the back of a spoon to make sure the chocolate fills in all of the mold and up the edges. Refrigerate 10 minutes to set. If the edges are thin, carefully brush more chocolate around the edges and refrigerate for 5 more minutes. Carefully unmold. Set aside 6 of the shells for the tops. Melt the edges of 6 of the shells that will be the bottoms. Fill these cocoa bomb shells with: 1 tablespoon white hot cocoa mix and a handful of mini marshmallows. Melt the edges of the leftover shells and attach the tops. Let set.

Meanwhile, thoroughly mix the 2 ounces orange candy melts and the 1 ounce white candy melts to create a nice light orange color, if using. Fill one small piping bag or plastic bag with the orange chocolate, and one with the other 2 ounces of white candy chocolate. When ready to decorate, snip off a very small amount of the orange piping bag tip and pipe diagonal lines across the hearts. Then switch to the white piping bag, snip off a small amount of the tip, and pipe across the hearts on the opposite diagonal. Sprinkle with gold and white sugar pearls. Let set.

To Make: Place a hot cocoa bomb in the bottom of a mug. Add 8–10 ounces of very hot milk and stir well. Drink to the ladies who brunch with you . . . in "real clothes" or in pajamas.

Raspberry-Rose Beret Cocoa Bombs

This is one of my favorite cocoa bombs in this book, because it tastes so unique and gloriously extravagant. Raspberry! Rose! Chocolate! Macarons! Swoooooooon. It's like a day at the spa and a tea at the Ritz combined, and it's topped with a little pink "beret" mini macaron. The mini macarons are just the perfect topper and the pink roses make these ideal for a galentine's day event. The mini macarons will actually float in the implosion of the cocoa bomb, so you can even put an extra mini macaron inside if you are serving these immediately (macarons should usually be kept refrigerated). Feel free to add pink heart-shaped mini marshmallows, too. I highly recommend using a dab of melted chocolate to attach the mini macarons, as the edible glue remains tacky for too long and the macarons tend to slide off.

MAKES 6 REGULAR COCOA BOMBS

12 ounces milk chocolate candy melts *or* milk chocolate, tempered
1 teaspoon raspberry flavoring oil, or to taste
¾ teaspoon rose flavoring oil, or to taste
1 recipe batch hot cocoa mix (page 40) *or* ½ cup store-bought mix
Edible dried rose petals
Edible dried rose buds
Freeze-dried raspberries
6 mini raspberry macarons
Edible glue or extra melted chocolate, for decorating

Melt the chocolate and thoroughly stir in both flavoring oils to taste. Pour 1–2 tablespoons melted chocolate into each mold and use a brush or the back of a spoon to make sure the chocolate fills in all of the mold and up the edges. Refrigerate 5 minutes to set. If the edges are thin, carefully brush more chocolate around the edges and refrigerate for 5 more minutes. Carefully unmold. Set aside 6 of the shells for the tops. Melt the edges of 6 of the shells that will be the bottoms. Fill these cocoa bomb shells with: 1 tablespoon hot cocoa mix, a handful of dried rose petals, one or two dried rose buds, and a handful of freeze-dried raspberries. Melt the edges of the leftover shells and attach the tops. Let set. Before serving, brush a bit of edible glue or extra melted chocolate on the top of each cocoa bomb and top with a beautiful edible rose bud or mini raspberry macaron.

> **To Make:** Place a hot cocoa bomb in the bottom of a mug. Add 10 ounces of very hot milk and stir well. Sip and be transported to a beautiful café, sitting at a red-velvet banquette, surrounded by mirrors and flowers.

Spicy Sizzling Cocoa Bombs

Add a little spice to cold winter evenings with this sizzling Mexican-spiced hot cocoa. Notes of warm winter spices such as cinnamon, nutmeg, and a dash of cloves are standard, but a dash of cayenne really ups the ante. Use a specialty or dark cocoa mix for filling the cocoa bombs if you can find it, as it makes a really nice background for the spices and can stand up to their heat! The only question will be, can you stand up to the heat? Feel free to play with the measurements so this tastes juuuuuust right for you.

MAKES 6 REGULAR COCOA BOMBS

12 ounces milk chocolate candy
   melts *or* milk chocolate,
   tempered
1 tablespoon cinnamon, or to taste
½ teaspoon cayenne pepper, or to
   taste
¼ teaspoon nutmeg, or to taste
1 recipe batch hot cocoa mix (page
   40) *or* ½ cup store-bought mix
Edible glue, vegetable oil, or extra
   melted chocolate, for decorating
Cinnamon sticks, for decorating
1 cup dark cocoa powder, for
   decorating
½ teaspoon cayenne pepper, for
   decorating
A pinch red edible glitter, for
   decorating

Melt the chocolate and pour 1–2 tablespoons melted chocolate into each mold and use a brush or the back of a spoon to make sure the chocolate fills in all of the mold and up the edges. Refrigerate 5 minutes to set. If the edges are thin, carefully brush more chocolate around the edges and refrigerate for 5 more minutes. Carefully unmold. Mix the hot cocoa mix with the 1 tablespoon cinnamon, ½ teaspoon cayenne pepper, and the ¼ teaspoon nutmeg. Set aside 6 of the shells for the tops. Melt the edges of 6 of the shells that will be the bottoms. Fill these cocoa bomb shells with 1 tablespoon spiced hot cocoa mix. Melt the edges of the leftover shells and attach the tops. Let set. To decorate, mix the 1 cup dark cocoa powder, ½ teaspoon cayenne pepper, and pinch of red glitter in a wide dish. Use a brush dipped in vegetable oil, melted cooled chocolate, or edible glue to cover the top of the cocoa bomb. Then dip it in the dark cocoa mixture, coating the top half. Cut a cinnamon stick in half using sharp scissors. Then use edible glue or extra melted chocolate to dip the cinnamon stick and secure to the back at an angle. Hold securely but lightly for at least 30 seconds then refrigerate until set. Repeat for all cocoa bombs.

To Make: Place a hot cocoa bomb in the bottom of a mug. Add 10 ounces of very hot milk and stir well. Feel the warmth of Mexico even in the depths of winter.

Easter Basket Cocoa Egg Bombs

Hollow chocolate eggs filled with marshmallow chicks and fun Easter surprises are just so delightful! Decorate these as you would decorate any Easter eggs . . . go all out and be creative with chocolate, sprinkles, edible glitter and more. Make each one different if you want! Any color candy melts or colored chocolate work, too, to create edible decorated easter eggs. I love the taste of dark chocolate and how it lets the decorations stand out, but kids might be more inclined towards milk or white chocolate. I highly recommend getting a polycarbonate mold for your egg-shaped cocoa bombs, as the two halves actually fit together to make a true egg shape. The silicone molds are far too deep and oddly-shaped to put together and create a normal-looking egg shape!

MAKES 6 REGULAR COCOA BOMBS

12 ounces dark chocolate candy melts *or* dark chocolate, tempered
1 recipe batch hot cocoa mix (page 40) *or* ½ cup store-bought mix
Dehydrated mini marshmallows
6 edible marshmallow chicks
Spring/Easter-themed sprinkles and sugar, such as chicks and eggs, flowers, birds, and brightly colored sanding sugar
2 ounces extra chocolate (color of your choice) for decorating

Melt the chocolate and pour 1–2 tablespoons melted chocolate into each mold and use a brush or the back of a spoon to make sure the chocolate fills in all of the mold and up the edges. Refrigerate 5 minutes to set. If the edges are thin, carefully brush more chocolate around the edges and refrigerate for 5 more minutes. Carefully unmold. Set aside 6 of the shells for the tops. Melt the edges of 6 of the shells that will be the bottoms. Fill these cocoa bomb shells with 1 tablespoon hot cocoa mix, a few mini marshmallows, and tuck one marshmallow chick on top. Melt the edges of the leftover shells and attach the tops. Let set. Decorate as you wish! In these photos I put colored chocolate in a piping bag, snipped the tip and piped lines, then added sanding sugar and spring-themed sprinkles.

To Make: Place a hot cocoa bomb in the bottom of a mug. Add 8–10 ounces of very hot milk and stir well. Wait for the chick to pop up and say hello to spring!

Sweet Spring Maple Cocoa Bombs

I love February in Vermont, believe it or not. It's the time the light shifts, the days start to get longer, and spring is on the horizon. Maple sugaring season is the very start of that, when the days are sunny and warm, and the nights are still cold. The sugar shacks around the state send woodsmoke into the now-bright-blue skies as they boil the sap down to syrup. It's a cheerful sight indeed. Maple sugar, made by continuing to boil the syrup until all the liquid evaporates, is a truly sweet treat. These cocoa bombs have maple sugar and maple sugar candies in them to bring that sweet spring sweetness to a cup of cocoa. Milk and dark chocolate are equally good with the maple filling!

MAKES 6 REGULAR COCOA BOMBS

12 ounces dark chocolate candy melts *or* dark chocolate, tempered
1 cup dark cocoa powder
¼–½ cup maple sugar, depending on taste
½ teaspoon salt
6–12 maple sugar candies, such as leaves
Edible glue or extra melted chocolate, for decorating

Melt the chocolate and pour 1–2 tablespoons melted chocolate into each mold and use a brush or the back of a spoon to make sure the chocolate fills in all of the mold and up the edges. Refrigerate 5 minutes to set. If the edges are thin, carefully brush more chocolate around the edges and refrigerate for 5 more minutes. Carefully unmold. Set aside 6 of the shells for the tops. Melt the edges of 6 of the shells that will be the bottoms. In a medium bowl, mix together the cocoa powder, maple sugar, and salt. Fill the cocoa bomb shells with 1 tablespoon hot cocoa mix and a maple sugar candy, if desired. Melt the edges of the leftover shells and attach the tops. Let set. Use a torch to lightly heat the top of the cocoa bombs one at a time or use a dab of edible glue or melted chocolate to attach a maple sugar candy to the top of each bomb.

To Make: Place a hot cocoa bomb in the bottom of a mug. Add 8–10 ounces of very hot milk and stir well. Sip that sweet late-winter nectar.

Key Lime Cocoa Bombs

If I could be a snowbird, I would in a heartbeat. My family lived in Florida for many years, and before that, we vacationed there often. Our first stop on vacation was always to pick up a key lime pie, the very essence of Florida in a dessert. I still love that tangy, cold, creamy pie, but I love the flavor of the tiny key limes (we could buy them at the farmer's market!) in just about anything nowadays, including hot cocoa. Key lime flavoring oil will give you the concentrated, truly key lime flavor that is very different from regular lime. It pairs perfectly with the simplicity of white chocolate.

MAKES 6 REGULAR COCOA BOMBS

12 ounces white chocolate candy melts *or* white chocolate, tempered
½–1 teaspoon key lime flavoring oil, to taste
1 recipe batch white cocoa mix (page 41) *or* ½ cup store-bought mix
Freeze-dried lime powder, optional
1 cup lime-flavored mini marshmallows
2 ounces light green candy melts *or* white chocolate, tempered and colored
Light green sanding sugar

Melt the chocolate and thoroughly stir in the flavoring oil to taste. Pour 1–2 tablespoons melted chocolate into the molds and use a brush or the back of a spoon to make sure the chocolate fills in all of the mold and up the edges. Refrigerate 5 minutes to set. If the edges are thin, carefully brush more chocolate around the edges and refrigerate for 5 more minutes. Carefully unmold. Set aside the 6 shells for the tops. Melt the edges of the shells that will be the bottoms. Fill these cocoa bomb shells with: 1 tablespoon white cocoa mix, a dash of lime powder, and a handful of marshmallows. Melt the edges of the top shells and attach the tops. Let set. Add the melted green chocolate to a piping bag or a plastic storage bag, and carefully cut off a small part of the tip. Pipe lines across the finished bombs. Sprinkle liberally with light green sanding sugar. Let set.

To Make: Place a hot cocoa bomb in the bottom of a mug. Add 8–10 ounces of very hot milk and stir well. Microwave for an additional 10–20 seconds, then stir well again. Pretend you are being warmed by the sun on a fine-sand beach you have *allllll* to yourself.

Chocolate-Covered Pineapple Cocoa Bombs

These cocoa bombs look like a party! It may sound unusual to have pineapple in hot chocolate, but trust me, it's a delicious flavor combination. Freeze-dried pineapple has a tropical look like sea sponge, but becomes fully pineapple fruity-ness once it is in the liquid. Combined with chocolate, this is a sweet, creamy, dreamy drink that's a bit of summer in the middle of winter. I happened to luck out and find these adorable hula drink skirts at a thrift store, but you could easily make your own.

MAKES 6 REGULAR COCOA BOMBS

- 6–8 ounces yellow candy melts *or* white chocolate, tempered and colored bright yellow
- 6–8 ounces dark chocolate candy melts *or* tempered dark chocolate
- ½ teaspoon pineapple flavoring oil, to taste
- 1 recipe batch hot cocoa mix (page 40) *or* ½ cup store-bought mix
- Freeze-dried pineapple pieces
- ½ cup mini marshmallows
- Pineapple sprinkles, optional
- 2 ounces yellow candy melts *or* tempered with chocolate with yellow food coloring oil, for decorating
- Extra melted chocolate for decorating

Melt the yellow chocolate and thoroughly stir in the flavoring oil to taste. Pour 1–2 tablespoons melted chocolate into 6 mold cavities and use a brush or the back of a spoon to make sure the chocolate fills in all of the mold and up the edges. Refrigerate 5 minutes to set. If the edges are thin, carefully brush more chocolate around the edges and refrigerate for 5 more minutes. Carefully unmold. Repeat the process with the dark chocolate, also filling 6 mold cavities, so you have 6 yellow halves and 6 dark chocolate halves. Set aside the 6 dark chocolate shells for the tops. Melt the edges of the yellow shells that will be the bottom. Fill these cocoa bomb shells with: 1 tablespoon hot cocoa mix, a few pineapple sprinkles, a few marshmallows, and a piece or two of freeze-dried pineapple. Melt the edges of the dark chocolate top shells and attach the tops. Let set. Spoon the yellow candy melts for decorating into a piping bag or a plastic storage bag, and carefully cut off a small part of the tip. Pipe lines across the finished bombs. Dip a few large pieces of freeze-dried pineapple in the extra melted chocolate and carefully place on top of each bomb. Let set.

To Make: Place a hot cocoa bomb in the bottom of a mug. Pineapple mugs are extra fun! Add 10 ounces of very hot milk and stir well. Microwave for an additional 10–20 seconds, then stir well again. Take a few sips, then practice your hula dancing.

Black and White Cookie Cocoa Bombs

Black and white cookies are soft cake-like cookies with half chocolate and half vanilla frosting. But I just had to take the name of this cookie a little too literally with the black and white halves for some pop-art–style fun photos. Nonetheless, these taste like the puffy round cookies, with sugar cookie flavoring added, and the black is actually chocolate with black coloring added. I added black sanding sugar to the white cocoa along with plenty of marshmallows to keep the black and white theme going on the inside of the bomb, but feel free to skip that if you don't have any handy. White cocoa mix lets you really taste the flavor, but once again, regular cocoa mix tastes great too!

MAKES 6 REGULAR COCOA BOMBS

8 ounces milk or dark chocolate candy melts *or* milk or dark chocolate, tempered
8 ounces white candy melts *or* white chocolate, tempered
Black oil-based food coloring, if desired
1 teaspoon sugar cookie flavoring oil, to taste, divided
1 recipe batch white cocoa mix (page 41) *or* ½ cup store-bought mix
1 cup dehydrated mini marshmallows
Black sanding sugar, optional

Melt the 8 ounces milk or dark chocolate and add ½ teaspoon of the flavoring oil and mix thoroughly. Add a few drops of black oil-based food coloring if desired and stir thoroughly until the chocolate is black. Pour 1–2 tablespoons black chocolate into each mold and use a brush or the back of a spoon to make sure the chocolate fills in all of the mold and up the edges. Refrigerate 5 minutes to set. If the edges are thin, carefully brush more chocolate around the edges and refrigerate for 5 more minutes. Carefully unmold. Repeat the process with the white chocolate, adding the additional ½ teaspoon flavoring oil but no coloring. Set aside 6 of the shells for the tops. Melt the edges of 6 of the shells that will be the bottoms. Fill these cocoa bomb shells with 1 tablespoon white cocoa mix, a liberal amount of mini marshmallows, and black sanding sugar, if desired. Melt the edges of the leftover shells and attach the tops. Let set.

To Make: Admire how shiny these two-toned orbs are, and how they remind you of billiard balls, or Magic 8 balls. Place a hot cocoa bomb in the bottom of a mug. Add 10 ounces of very hot milk and stir well. Now be glad it tastes like a black and white cookie, and not a billiard ball or a Magic 8 ball *(ewww)*.

Luck of the Irish Cocoa Bombs

Whoever receives one of these cocoa bombs will be flush with luck and sweet surprises! Not only are there treats inside, there's a rainbow landing on the gently sparkling Emerald Isle grass and a truly spectacular miniature pot of gold. These cocoa bombs are sure to impress. I like to add crème de menthe flavoring oil, but feel free to leave it out.

MAKES 6 REGULAR COCOA BOMBS

12 ounces milk or dark chocolate candy melts *or* milk or dark chocolate, tempered
½–1 teaspoon crème de menthe flavoring oil, to taste
Miniature peanut butter cups, one for the top of each cocoa bomb plus more for inside if desired
Edible glue
Edible gold glitter
Gold metallic dragées
1 recipe batch white (page 41) or regular cocoa mix (page 40) *or* ½ cup store-bought mix
Four-leaf clover sprinkles, green metallic dragées, etc. for interior decorations
1 cup miniature dehydrated cereal-style marshmallows
3-D rainbow sugar or fondant decorations, one for the top of each cocoa bomb plus more for inside if desired
Chocolate coins, if desired
Edible green glitter
2 ounces light green candy melts *or* white chocolate, tempered and colored

Melt the chocolate and thoroughly stir in the flavoring oil to taste. Pour 1–2 tablespoons melted chocolate into the molds and use a brush or the back of a spoon to make sure the chocolate fills in all of the mold and up the edges. Refrigerate 5 minutes to set. If the edges are thin, carefully brush more chocolate around the edges and refrigerate for 5 more minutes. Carefully unmold. Then make the miniature pots of gold. Top each miniature peanut butter cup with a generous dollop of edible glue, then liberally sprinkle gold powder on top and carefully "fill" the top with gold metallic dragées. Let set until thoroughly dry. Set aside the 6 shells for the tops. Melt the edges of the shells that will be the bottom. Fill these cocoa bomb shells with: 1 tablespoon cocoa mix, plenty of sprinkles, and a handful of marshmallows. Add an additional rainbow, chocolate coin, or miniature pot of gold if desired. Melt the edges of the top shells and attach the tops. Let set. Use a brush and more edible glue to lightly coat the top of each bomb then cover them with edible green glitter. Put the melted green chocolate in a small bowl and dip the bottom of a rainbow decoration liberally in the chocolate, and place on the top of a cocoa bomb slightly to the back center. Hold for at least 30 seconds, until stable, then immediately refrigerate to solidify. Repeat for all cocoa bombs. When solid, add more green chocolate "grass" at the bottom of the rainbow and use that to attach a miniature pot of gold. Refrigerate at least another 5 minutes to set.

To Make: Place a hot cocoa bomb in the bottom of a mug. Add 8–10 ounces of very hot milk and stir well. See what the luck of the Irish brings you, both in your cocoa bomb and in your life!

Robin's Egg Cocoa Bombs

These turquoise eggs just scream spring, don't you think? They are so beautiful it's almost hard to believe they're made to eat (well, drink). I highly recommend using a polycarbonate egg mold for these, as the silicone egg molds are too deep and create a very awkwardly-shaped egg unless you melt the edges down significantly. For speckled eggs, dip a stiff food-only brush in melted chocolate and use it to flick chocolate lightly on the finished eggs. I like the mix of so-shiny-it-looks-fake plus the traditionally-speckled "robin's egg." These are nestled in edible grass, but they look just as at-home in a ceramic egg basket, on real grass (look up how to easily grow real-grass baskets for Easter), or in brightly colored ramekins. These make super fun place settings for an Easter brunch as well!

MAKES 5 OR 6 EGG COCOA BOMBS

8 ounces light blue candy melts

4 ounces turquoise candy melts *or* 12 ounces white chocolate, tempered, colored robin's egg blue

1 recipe batch white cocoa mix (page 41) *or* ½ cup store-bought mix

½ cup dehydrated mini marshmallows

Robin's egg chocolates, if desired

2 ounces milk or dark chocolate candy melts or tempered chocolate, for decorating

Melt the chocolate and pour 1–2 tablespoons melted chocolate into each mold and use a brush or the back of a spoon to make sure the chocolate fills in all of the mold and up the edges. Refrigerate 5 minutes to set. If the edges are thin, carefully brush more chocolate around the edges and refrigerate for 5 more minutes. Carefully unmold. Set aside half of the shells for the tops. Melt the edges of the shells that will be the bottom. Fill these bottom cocoa bomb shells with: 1 tablespoon white cocoa mix, a handful of mini marshmallows, and a few robin's egg chocolates, if desired. Melt the edges of the leftover shells and attach. Let set. Melt the 2 ounces of milk or dark chocolate and use a stiff, dry, food-only brush to flick chocolate over the eggs. Let set.

To Make: Place a hot cocoa bomb in the bottom of a mug. Add 6–8 ounces of very hot milk and stir well. Microwave for another 10–20 seconds and stir well to completely mix ingredients. Drink in the warmth and fun of Spring on its way.

Chai Chocolate Bombs

Chai is so fantastic in the winter. All of the spices really get your blood pumping and keep you warm from the inside-out. Though typically enjoyed in tea, the warming, wintery spices of chai go well with either milk or dark chocolate shells, so I did some of each with this batch. You could also fill these with an instant chai latte drink mix if you have one on hand. Everyone likes their chai spices a bit different, so experiment and get the perfect mix for your taste, or use a ready-made mixture and add ¼–½ teaspoon to each cocoa bomb.

MAKES 6 REGULAR COCOA BOMBS

10–12 ounces milk or dark chocolate wafers *or* 12 ounces milk or dark chocolate, tempered
1 recipe batch hot cocoa mix (page 40) *or* ½ cup store-bought mix
½ teaspoon *each*: cinnamon, nutmeg, cardamom, ginger, black pepper, allspice, ground cloves
½ cup dehydrated mini marshmallows, if desired
6 (1-ounce) squares of chai-flavored chocolate, optional

Melt the chocolate and pour 1–2 tablespoons melted chocolate into each mold and use a brush or the back of a spoon to make sure the chocolate fills in all of the mold and up the edges. Refrigerate 5 minutes to set. If the edges are thin, carefully brush more chocolate around the edges and refrigerate for 5 more minutes. Carefully unmold. Set aside half of the shells for the tops. Melt the edges of the shells that will be the bottom. In a small bowl, mix all of the spices. Fill these bottom cocoa bomb shells with: 1 tablespoon hot cocoa mix, ¼ teaspoon–½ teaspoon of the spice mixture, a handful of mini marshmallows, and a square of the chai chocolate, if desired. Melt the edges of the leftover shells and attach. Let set.

To Make: Place a hot cocoa bomb in the bottom of a mug. Add 6–8 ounces of very hot milk and stir well. Microwave for another 10–20 seconds and stir well to completely mix ingredients. Drink in the warmth of the exotic and yet familiar spices.

Chocolate-Spruce Forest Walk Cocoa Bombs

This cocoa bomb recipe is from my friends at Tavernier Chocolates in Brattleboro, Vermont. Their stand at the Brattleboro Farmers Market is a tiny haven filled with chocolate revelations. John and Dar have graciously shared this incredible recipe below. Dar says, "My father planted spruce trees along the perimeter of our property and an early memory is popping off the tender, light green spruce tips in the spring and eating them, the citrus-y resinous flavor waking up my senses like all of the flowers budding. Later on I learned that spruce is high in vitamin C, and that Native American peoples used spruce as medicine for respiratory complaints. I love pairing spruce with mint, two aromatic spices that are powerhouses of flavor and medicinal properties in traditional practices, and both grow in our Northern forests." This recipe makes twice as many as most in the book, since we know you'll want to share!

MAKES 15 OR 16 COCOA BOMBS (CUT THE RECIPE IN HALF IF DESIRED!)

22–24 ounces dark chocolate candy melts *or* dark chocolate, tempered
1 cup cocoa powder
1 cup ground dark chocolate or chocolate chips (use the best you can find!)
2 tablespoons ground dried mint*
1 tablespoon ground dried spruce needles**
16 small pure maple sugar candies (such as small maple leaves)

*It will take roughly 4x as much whole dried mint and 2x as much whole dried spruce needle to get the above measurements.

** Only use wild or farmed spruce needles (not tips) that you are sure have not been sprayed by pesticides, anti-desiccants, or other chemicals (so not spruce from your Christmas wreath!). Make sure they are thoroughly cleaned and dried before using. You can get culinary spruce needles that are ready to use online; we love Halifax Hollow's Vermont wildcrafted spruce. Grind the mint and spruce fresh in a spice mill or coffee mill (be aware that you will make your coffee mill smell like spruce and mint and their strong aromas will flavor your coffee beans for a few grinds to come!). It will take roughly 4x as much whole dried mint and 2x as much whole dried spruce needle to get the above measurements.

You may need to make the shells in several batches if you only have one set of molds. Melt the chocolate and pour 1–2 tablespoons melted chocolate into each mold and use a brush or the back of a spoon to make sure the chocolate fills in all of the mold and up the edges. Refrigerate 5 minutes to set. If the edges are thin, carefully brush more chocolate around the edges and refrigerate for 5 more minutes. Unmold the shells and let them come to room temperature. Set aside half of the shells as tops. Melt the edges of the bottom six halves. In a medium bowl, mix together the cocoa powder, ground chocolate, ground dried mint, and ground spruce needles. Place 2 tablespoons in the bottom of each shell. Top with a small maple candy. Melt the edges of the leftover shells and attach the tops. Let set.

To Make: Place a hot cocoa bomb in the bottom of a mug. Add 8 ounces of very hot milk and stir well. If you're not into the texture of the spruce needles, you can allow them to steep for a few minutes to infuse the flavor into the hot milk and then strain out the needles. This drink is perfect for apres-ski, in front of a fireplace, a morning winter cup to wake up, or in a thermos on a snowy hike.

Dragon Fruit Power Pink Cocoa Bombs

Dragon fruit has been exploding onto the power food scene lately. What makes it a power food? It is packed with antioxidants, vitamins, minerals, and prebiotics. The spunky magenta and green fruit is actually the berry of a cactus. The interior flesh is white or deep purple with black seeds, reminiscent of a black and white kiwi. The flavor of this pink-purple heart bomb is also reminiscent of a sweet drink put out by a famous coffee shop a few summers ago. The dragon fruit flavor is slightly floral, a little bit fruity, and the milk adds a complementary creaminess. A few grains of salt (seriously, don't overdo it) really brings out the flavor. Speaking of the flavor, I tried adding freeze-dried dragon fruit to this bomb, but don't do it! The fruit is extremely concentrated and bitter when freeze-dried so I don't recommend that, despite the pretty pink color it adds. If you're looking for a freeze-dried fruit to add, try pear or strawberry, both flavors that complement the dragon fruit.

MAKES 6–8 HEART COCOA BOMBS

8 ounces purple candy melts
2 ounces white candy melts
2 ounces light pink candy melts
**   or 12 ounces white chocolate,**
**   tempered, colored purple-pink**
¼ teaspoon dragon fruit flavoring
**   oil, or to taste**
1 recipe batch white cocoa mix
**   (page 41) or ½ cup store-bought**
**   mix**
2 teaspoons dragon fruit (pitaya)
**   powder**
Few grains salt
½ cup dehydrated mini
**   marshmallows**
2 ounces bright pink candy melts or
**   white chocolate, tempered and**
**   colored bright pink**
Edible pink or purple glitter or
**   luster dust**

Melt the chocolate and thoroughly stir in the flavoring oil to taste. Pour 1–2 tablespoons melted chocolate into each mold and use a brush or the back of a spoon to make sure the chocolate fills in all of the mold and up the edges. Refrigerate 5 minutes to set. If the edges are thin, carefully brush more chocolate around the edges and refrigerate for 5 more minutes. Carefully unmold. Set aside half of the shells for the tops. Melt the edges of the shells that will be the bottoms. Fill these bottom cocoa bomb shells with: 1 tablespoon white cocoa mix, ⅛–¼ teaspoon dragon fruit powder, a few grains of salt, and a handful of mini marshmallows. Melt the edges of the leftover shells and attach. Let set. Melt the 2 ounces of pink candy melts and use a spoon to drizzle it over the tops of the cocoa bombs. Immediately use your fingers or a brush to flick the edible glitter on the pink candy melts. Let set.

To Make: Place a hot cocoa bomb in the bottom of a mug. Add 8–10 ounces of very hot milk and stir well. Microwave for another 10–20 seconds and stir well to completely mix ingredients. Feel all that good pink power strength infuse you with dragon vibes. You are powerful and beautiful.

Love Elixir Cacao Bomb
(Cacao Maca Rose)

My friend Jessica Jean Weston is a knowledge powerhouse when it comes to plant-based foods and medicine. She owns Superfresh! Café in downtown Brattleboro, Vermont and is the author of Healing Tonics, Juices, and Smoothies. *Jessica says, "This is basically my favorite superfood hot chocolate both at home and at my restaurant, in hot chocolate bomb form. The outer shell made with raw cacao butter makes the most delicious velvety, frothy, thick hot chocolate. After cacao, maca is probably my next favorite superfood. Grown in the high Andes of Peru, maca is a root vegetable that we see here in dried, powdered form and is available at almost every health food store or food co-op, along with raw cacao powder. Maca has a sweet and slightly malty flavor and is most known as a powerful adaptogen. It can also increase energy and endurance. Both maca and cacao are known as aphrodisiacs, making them the perfect pair with rose for the ultimate love elixir."*

MAKES 6 REGULAR COCOA BOMBS

Shell:
3.25 ounces raw cacao butter
½ cup raw cacao powder
¼ cup Vermont maple syrup (or liquid sweetener of choice)
Pinch salt

Filling:
¾ cup raw cacao powder
¼ cup maca powder
1 tablespoon + 2 teaspoons rose petal dust or powder*, plus extra for decorating
6 tablespoons coconut sugar**

*You can make your own rose petal dust by processing dried rose petals in a spice grinder, high speed blender, or mortar & pestle.

**You can swap coconut sugar for any granular sugar if you prefer (brown sugar, raw cane, etc.), or leave out for a lower sugar content.

Add the raw cacao butter to your double boiler (see page 9 for making your own) and melt on medium heat. Once the cacao butter is melted, turn off heat and add the raw cacao powder, maple syrup, and a pinch of salt. Stir or whisk until it is well incorporated. In a small mixing bowl, whisk together all of the filling ingredients, making sure there are no clumps. Then use the back of a spoon or a food-safe brush to add 1 teaspoon or so of the shell mixture to your chocolate bomb molds, evenly coating the edges as best you can. Make sure there are no holes and that you get it covered all the way to the top edge. Place in the freezer on a flat surface for 10–20 minutes. Add a second coat to the shell and put back in the freezer. If it looks a bit thin, add a third coat and put back in the freezer until solid (about 10 minutes). Very carefully remove the chocolate shells from their molds. Fill each the 6 chocolate shell halves that will be the bottoms with 3 tablespoons of filling mixture. Very gently and quickly warm the edges of the top shells and attach. Use your finger to gently help melted chocolate cover any gaps and stick together well. To decorate, drizzle the top of the chocolate bombs with extra chocolate sauce left over from the shell and sprinkle with rose petal dust.

To Make: Place the hot chocolate bomb in your favorite *big* mug (Jessica and I love the handmade mugs she uses in the café, made by Z Pots!), pour 8–10 ounces of your favorite hot plant-based mylk over top and stir to enjoy!

North Forest Spice
(Cacao Chaga Cinnamon Ginger)

Here is the second recipe from Jessica, inspired by foraging in our woods and the amazing health benefits of mushroom powders. "Chaga is known as the 'king of medicinal mushrooms' and grows primarily on birch trees in colder climates of the Northern Hemisphere. It is used for immune support and longevity. Chaga can be found in most health food stores and food co-ops, usually in bulk. I always look for locally sourced, sustainable sources as this is a mushroom that tends to be improperly/over harvested. Feel free to swap other mushroom powders in its place (reishi, lion's mane, cordyceps, shiitake, etc.). Adding to the immune support are two classic spices, cinnamon and ginger, both offering warming and anti-inflammatory support. This is the perfect hot chocolate for those extra-cold winter days."

MAKES 6 REGULAR COCOA BOMBS

Shell:
3.25 ounces raw cacao butter
½ cup raw cacao powder
¼ cup Vermont maple syrup (or liquid sweetener of choice)
2 teaspoons cinnamon powder
Pinch salt

Filling:
¾ cup raw cacao powder
2 teaspoons ginger powder
4 teaspoons finely ground chaga mushroom powder
6 tablespoons coconut sugar**

Garnish:
2 tablespoons finely grated fresh ginger root OR powdered dried ginger

**You can swap coconut sugar for any granular sugar if you prefer (brown sugar, raw cane, etc.), or leave out for a lower sugar content.

To Make: Place the hot chocolate bomb in your favorite big mug, pour your favorite hot plant-based mylk over top and stir to enjoy!

Add the raw cacao butter to your double boiler (see page 9 for making your own) and melt on medium heat. Once cacao butter is melted, turn off heat and add raw cacao powder, maple syrup, cinnamon, and a pinch of salt. Stir or whisk until it is well incorporated. In a small mixing bowl, whisk together all filling ingredients, making sure there are no clumps. Using the back of a spoon or food-safe brush, add 1 teaspoon of the shell mixture to your chocolate bomb molds, evenly coating the edges as best you can. Make sure there are no holes and that you get it covered all the way to the top edge. Place in the freezer on a flat surface for 10–20 minutes. Add a second coat to the shell and put back in the freezer. If it looks a bit thin, add a third coat and put back in the freezer until solid (about 10 minutes). Very carefully, remove the chocolate shells from their molds. Fill each of the 6 chocolate shell halves that will be the bottoms with 3 tablespoons of the filling mixture. Very gently and quickly warm the edges of the top halves of the chocolate shells and attach. Use your finger to gently help melted chocolate cover any gaps and stick together well. To decorate, drizzle the top of the chocolate bombs with extra chocolate sauce leftover from the shell and sprinkle with grated or dried ginger to garnish.

Lucuma Loca White Chocolate Bomb
(White Chocolate Wild Orange Lucuma)

Also from Jessica, this recipe is a truly inspiring one. She says, "Let's brighten things up with a little bit of sweet and a burst of citrus! Lucuma is a fruit native to Peru with a natural sweetness, often used as a sweetener alternative. Just like maca, we get lucuma in dried powdered form here in the US. Lucuma powder can be found at almost every health food store and food coop. To bring in the wild orange flavor, I used fresh orange zest in the filling and garnish, along with food-grade wild orange essential oil in the shell and filling."

NOTE: Not all essential oils are safe for internal use! Please do not use just any essential oil, *only* a food-grade one. Jessica loves to use dōTERRA® oils.

Makes 6 regular cocoa bombs

Shell:
- 3.25 ounces raw cacao butter
- ¼ cup raw cashew butter (or macadamia butter)*
- 3 tablespoons Vermont maple syrup (or liquid sweetener of choice)
- 4 drops *food-grade* wild orange essential oil, optional

Filling:
- 6 tablespoons lucuma powder
- 2 tablespoons fresh orange zest
- 4 drops *food-grade* wild orange essential oil, optional
- 6 tablespoons coconut sugar**

Garnish:
- 3 tablespoons fresh orange zest

*This recipe has to use a very light colored nut or seed butter. Coconut manna might work as a nut-free alternative.

**You can swap coconut sugar for any granular sugar if you prefer (brown sugar, raw cane, etc.), or leave out for a lower sugar content.

Add the raw cacao butter to your double boiler (see page 9 for making your own) and melt on medium heat. Once the cacao butter is melted, add the raw cashew butter, maple syrup, and wild orange essential oil (if using). Stir until it is well incorporated and cashew butter has softened. In a small mixing bowl, whisk together all filling ingredients, making sure there are no clumps. Using the back of a spoon or food-safe brush, add 1 teaspoon of the shell mixture to your chocolate bomb molds, evenly coating the edges as best you can. Make sure there are no holes and that you get it covered all the way to the top edge. Place in the freezer on a flat surface for 10–20 minutes. Repeat this step 4–5 times to get a thick enough coat. This shell batter does not like to stay up the edges as much without powder in the ingredient list. If you prefer, you can add a few tablespoons of powdered coconut milk or powdered sugar. Very carefully remove the shells from their molds. Fill each of the 6 chocolate shell halves that will be the bottoms with 3 tablespoons of the filling mixture. Very gently and quickly warm the edges of the empty halves of the chocolate shells and attach. Use your finger to gently help melted chocolate cover any gaps and stick together well. To decorate, drizzle the tops of the chocolate bombs with extra white chocolate sauce leftover from the shell and garnish with orange zest.

To Make: Place the hot chocolate bomb in your favorite *big* mug, pour your favorite *hot* plant-based mylk over top, and stir to enjoy!

Hazelnut Dream Cocoa Bombs

This creamy, chocolately, hazelnut-y cocoa bomb is sure to be a favorite for chocolate lovers of all ages. My husband's good college friend came to our wedding with his wife and their two young boys, and we gifted them a jar of the classic hazelnut cocoa spread that was bigger than both of the boys' heads. They screamed with delight! I wonder how long it took them to go through that giant jar . . . I know it wouldn't take me very long! Hazelnut cocoa spread is addictive, and is rich enough to create a creamy hot chocolate without any additional powder. I have also added a secret little hazelnut gem! I used a silicone "flame" mold, but you can use any shape you have on hand, as long as a hazelnut will fit inside and be fully surrounded by chocolate. If you don't want to make your own, feel free to add a store-bought chocolate with a hazelnut filling.

MAKES 6 REGULAR COCOA BOMBS

12 ounces milk chocolate candy melts *or* milk chocolate, tempered
¾ cup hazelnut cocoa spread
4–6 ounces dark chocolate candy melts *or* dark chocolate, tempered
12 full hazelnuts, plus extra for decorating
½ cup dehydrated mini marshmallows

Warning: Whole hazelnuts may be a choking hazard. Avoid using whole hazelnuts for children or anyone prone to choking. If gifting these cocoa bombs, include a note of caution.

Melt the chocolate. Pour 1–2 tablespoons melted chocolate into each mold and use a brush or the back of a spoon to make sure the chocolate fills in all of the mold and up the edges. Refrigerate 5 minutes to set. If the edges are thin, carefully brush more chocolate around the edges and refrigerate for 5 more minutes. Carefully unmold. Next, melt the 4–6 ounces of dark chocolate, and fill a silicone flame-shaped mold. Press a full hazelnut into each full mold, covering it over with the chocolate. Refrigerate for 30 minutes. Once solid, unmold the chocolates. Set aside 6 of the shells for the tops. Melt the edges of 6 of the shells that will be the bottoms. Fill these cocoa bomb shells with: 2 tablespoons of hazelnut-cocoa spread, a chocolate with a hazelnut inside, and a handful of mini marshmallows. Melt the edges of the leftover shells and attach the tops to bottoms. Let set. Use a brush with a bit of melted chocolate or a dab of edible glue and sprinkle with some chopped hazelnuts.

To Make: Place a hot cocoa bomb in the bottom of a mug. Add 8–10 ounces of very hot milk and stir well. Feel great that you are only eating one serving of hazelnut spread. Put the jar away. Put. The. Jar. Away.

Chocolate-Dipped Strawberry Cocoa Bombs

Chocolate-dipped strawberries are one of the treasures of February, that last edge of winter when the light starts to change and love is in the air. If you've ever visited Florida in February, you know that strawberries are in season and the talk of the town. Strawberry festivals abound, and the scent of spring in Florida is definitely sweet, ripe, red strawberries! This hot chocolate evokes all of those wonderful, spring-like feelings that love always inspires, as chocolate-dipped strawberries are a sure sign of romance. There are several creative options with this recipe, too. Feel free to use strawberry Nesquick in place of the hot cocoa mix, or to use red candy melts for both or half of the shells. You can also use white cocoa mix inside with a pinch of red powdered food coloring. No matter which way you make it, this is a winning combination!

MAKES 6 REGULAR COCOA BOMBS

10 ounces dark chocolate candy melts *or* dark chocolate, tempered
½ teaspoon strawberry flavor oil, or to taste
1 recipe batch hot cocoa mix (page 40) *or* ½ cup store-bought mix
Freeze-dried strawberries
½ cup dehydrated mini marshmallows *or* pink mini marshmallows
A very small amount of dark chocolate, melted, *or* edible glue, for decorating

Melt the chocolate and thoroughly stir in the flavoring oil to taste. Pour 1–2 tablespoons melted chocolate into each mold and use a brush or the back of a spoon to make sure the chocolate fills in all of the mold and up the edges. Refrigerate 5 minutes to set. If the edges are thin, carefully brush more chocolate around the edges and refrigerate for 5 more minutes. Carefully unmold. Set aside 6 of the shells for the tops. Melt the edges of 6 of the shells that will be the bottoms. Fill these cocoa bomb shells with: 1 tablespoon hot cocoa mix, a handful of freeze-dried strawberries, and a handful of mini marshmallows. Melt the edges of the leftover shells and attach the tops to bottoms. Let set. Use a brush with a bit of melted chocolate or a dab of edible glue to attach a beautiful piece of bright red (hopefully heart-shaped!) freeze-dried strawberry on to each bomb.

To Make: Place a hot cocoa bomb in the bottom of a mug. Add 10 ounces of very hot milk and stir well. Best enjoyed with a handful of strawberries fresh from Florida in February.

Amaretto Cocoa Bombs

Amaretto is an under-rated, slightly bitter almond flavor, usually in liqueur form. I love anything almond-flavored, so amaretto is a big yes from me! Of course, this hot cocoa can be made an adult beverage with a splash of amaretto liqueur if you'd like. Whipped cream and a few ground almonds wouldn't be amiss either! Feel free to make these with either milk or dark chocolate shells; they both go nicely with the amaretto flavoring. You could also add slivered almonds, but since I choked on one in high school I'm not particularly keen to add them to a drink!

MAKES 6 REGULAR COCOA BOMBS

10 ounces dark chocolate candy melts *or* dark chocolate, tempered
½ teaspoon Amaretto flavor oil, or to taste
1 recipe batch hot cocoa mix (page 40) *or* ½ cup store-bought mix
½ cup dehydrated mini marshmallows
2 ounces white candy melts *or* white chocolate, tempered, for decorating
White seed pearl sprinkles, or similar, for decorating

Melt the chocolate and thoroughly stir in the flavoring oil to taste. Pour 1–2 tablespoons melted chocolate into each mold and use a brush or the back of a spoon to make sure the chocolate fills in all of the mold and up the edges. Refrigerate 5 minutes to set. If the edges are thin, carefully brush more chocolate around the edges and refrigerate for 5 more minutes. Carefully unmold. Set aside 6 of the shells for the tops. Melt the edges of 6 of the shells that will be the bottoms. Fill these cocoa bomb shells with: 1 tablespoon hot cocoa mix and a handful of mini marshmallows. Melt the edges of the leftover shells and attach the tops to bottoms. Let set. Melt the 2 ounces of white chocolate and add to a piping bag with a very fine tip or a plastic bag and snip the corner to create a very small opening. Pipe lines across tops of cocoa bombs in both directions. Add a generous sprinkle of white seed pearl sprinkles.

To Make: Place a hot cocoa bomb in the bottom of a mug. Add 10 ounces of very hot milk and stir well. Add a large cloud of whipped cream and drizzle amaretto liqueur through it if you're in the mood!

Orange-Chocolate Cocoa Bombs

The aroma of hot chocolate and fresh orange is intoxicating in the depths of winter. The orange flavor oil mixes with the dark chocolate really well. Feel free to use milk chocolate instead, of course! Most of us are familiar with the chocolate oranges available around the holidays; you have to knock them against the table nice and hard to separate the "orange" slices. I don't know how they make these, but I'm glad they do! As you can see, I snuck one of these bombs in the orange bowl at breakfast; I think since it has fruit in it, it can count as a breakfast drink, right?

MAKES 6 REGULAR COCOA BOMBS

10 ounces dark chocolate candy melts *or* dark chocolate, tempered

½–1 teaspoon orange flavor oil, or to taste

1 recipe batch hot cocoa mix (page 40) *or* ½ cup store-bought mix

½ cup dehydrated mini marshmallows *or* orange mini marshmallows

2 ounces orange candy melts *or* white chocolate, tempered and colored orange

Chocolate orange slices, for decorating, if desired

Melt the chocolate and thoroughly stir in the flavoring oil to taste. Pour 1–2 ablespoons melted chocolate into each mold and use a brush or the back of a spoon to make sure the chocolate fills in all of the mold and up the edges. Refrigerate 5 minutes to set. If the edges are thin, carefully brush more chocolate around the edges and refrigerate for 5 more minutes. Carefully unmold. Set aside 6 of the shells for the tops. Melt the edges of 6 of the shells that will be the bottoms. Fill these cocoa bomb shells with: 1 tablespoon hot cocoa mix and a handful of mini marshmallows. Melt the edges of the leftover shells and attach the tops to bottoms. Let set. Melt the 2 ounces of orange chocolate and add to a piping bag with a very fine tip or a plastic bag and snip the corner to create a very small opening. Pipe lines across one direction. Serve each cocoa bomb with a chocolate orange slice.

To Make: Place a hot cocoa bomb in the bottom of a mug. Add 8–10 ounces of very hot milk and stir well. Once the end of January sets in, you can find Cara Cara or Raspberry oranges in the grocery store; they're utterly delicious and a great fresh snack to eat with this hot cocoa.

Coffee and Chocolate Forever Cocoa Bombs

Mocha—that delightful blend of coffee and chocolate—will forever be a classic flavor combination. My family is Swedish, so we are coffee lovers by our heritage and proud of it. Filling this cocoa bomb with coffee and cocoa mix, along with a little creamer powder, creates a delicious mocha that can be enjoyed any time of day. Stroopwafels are a Dutch treat consisting of two very thin cookies sandwiched with a honey or caramel filling, and set over a steaming cup of coffee or tea to melt the filling. You then dip or dunk the softened cookie in the coffee.

MAKES 6 REGULAR COCOA BOMBS

- 10–12 ounces dark chocolate candy melts *or* dark chocolate, tempered
- 1 recipe batch hot cocoa mix (page 40) *or* ½ cup store-bought mix
- 6 teaspoons instant coffee
- 6 teaspoons instant French vanilla coffee creamer
- ½ cup dehydrated mini marshmallows *or* orange mini marshmallows
- 12 mini stroopwafels, honey or caramel filled
- Chocolate-covered espresso beans
- Edible glue or extra melted chocolate, for decorating

Melt the chocolate and pour 1–2 tablespoons melted chocolate into each mold and use a brush or the back of a spoon to make sure the chocolate fills in all of the mold and up the edges. Refrigerate 5 minutes to set. If the edges are thin, carefully brush more chocolate around the edges and refrigerate for 5 more minutes. Carefully unmold. Set aside 6 of the shells for the tops. Melt the edges of 6 of the shells that will be the bottoms. Fill these cocoa bomb shells with: 1 tablespoon hot cocoa mix, a teaspoon of instant coffee, a teaspoon of coffee creamer, and a handful of mini marshmallows. Add a mini stroopwafel and a few chocolate-covered espresso beans. Melt the edges of the leftover shells and attach the tops to bottoms. Let set. Use a bit of edible glue or extra melted chocolate to attach a mini stroopwafel to the top of each cocoa bomb, and a chocolate-covered espresso bean on top of that. Too cute!

To Make: Place a hot cocoa bomb in the bottom of a mug. Add approximately 10 ounces of very hot milk and stir well. Microwave for an extra 20 seconds to thoroughly combine ingredients and stir well again. Now call your mom or grandma, as the Swedes always talk to family while drinking coffee!

Chocoholic Cocoa Bombs

These cocoa bombs are a larger 3-inch size because the chocoholic cocoa bomb has to be bigger, right? I used dark chocolate to be a good deep base for the fillings, but feel free to use milk chocolate, too. No chocolate is left behind, here. I prefer to use a nice dark, specialty cocoa mix here as well. Don't forget brownie brittle, chocolate marshmallows, chocolate sprinkles, and mini chocolate chips. I mean, does it get any better than this? Oh yes, it does. I added gold-glittered chocolate shavings on top. You're welcome.

MAKES 6–8 (3-INCH) COCOA BOMBS

20–24 ounces dark or milk chocolate wafers *or* dark or milk chocolate, tempered
1 cup dark/extra-rich hot cocoa mix
Chocolate or chocolate chip marshmallows
Mini chocolate chips
Chocolate brownie brittle pieces
Chocolate jimmies/sprinkles
1 cup finely shaved chocolate, milk or dark
Gold edible glitter
Edible glue or extra melted chocolate, for decorating

Melt the chocolate and pour 1–2 tablespoons melted chocolate into each mold and use a brush or the back of a spoon to make sure the chocolate fills in all of the mold and up the edges. Refrigerate 5 minutes to set. If the edges are thin, carefully brush more chocolate around the edges and refrigerate for 5 more minutes. Carefully unmold. Set aside 6 of the shells for the tops. Melt the edges of 6 of the shells that will be the bottoms. Fill these cocoa bomb shells with: 1 tablespoon hot cocoa mix, a few chocolate marshmallows, mini chocolate chips, brownie brittle pieces, and chocolate sprinkles. Melt the edges of the leftover shells and attach the tops to bottoms. Let set. Use a bit of edible glue or extra melted chocolate to lightly coat the tops of the cocoa bombs. In a small bowl, mix the chocolate shavings and about a teaspoon of edible gold glitter, mixing thoroughly. Now coat each cocoa bomb top with the gilded chocolate shavings. Let set.

To Make: Place a hot cocoa bomb in the bottom of a mug. Add approximately 10 ounces of very hot milk and stir well. Microwave for an extra 20 seconds to thoroughly combine ingredients and stir well again. Revel in chocolate goodness.

Cookie Dough Cocoa Bombs

This cocoa bomb is perfect for the whole family, since we never outgrow a love of chocolate chip cookies! Movie theatre-style boxes of chocolate-dipped cookie dough bites are a fun addition to these cocoa bombs, as are mini chocolate chips. The fact that they look like balls of cookie dough is just too fun, too! This effect is easily achieved by using regular chocolate to paint chocolate chip "dots" on the mold and refrigerate those dots first, before gently adding nearly-cooled caramel-colored "cookie dough." You'll get compliments galore on these super-fun cocoa bombs that taste just like not-yet-baked chocolate chip cookie dough! I like to keep these simple and not add any additional decorations since they are so eye-catching already, but feel free to decorate more if you'd like!

Makes 6 regular cocoa bombs

2 ounces milk chocolate candy wafers *or* milk chocolate, tempered
12 ounces white candy melts colored caramel *or* white chocolate, tempered, colored caramel
½–1 teaspoon brown sugar flavoring oil, to taste
¼–½ teaspoon sugar cookie flavoring oil, to taste
1 recipe batch hot cocoa mix (page 40) *or* ½ cup store-bought mix
Cookie dough-flavored marshmallows *or* regular mini marshmallows
Miniature chocolate chips *and/ or* mini shelf-stable chocolate-covered cookie dough bites

Melt the milk chocolate and use a small, food-only brush to dot polka dots over each mold in random patterns, remembering to cover up to the very edge. Refrigerate at least 5 minutes. Meanwhile, melt the white chocolate and color it to your liking for a cookie dough color, then add the brown sugar and sugar cookie flavoring oils to taste. Let it cool until it is still liquid but not warm. Quickly pour 1–2 tablespoons melted chocolate into each mold and use a brush or the back of a spoon to make sure the chocolate fills in all of the mold and up the edges, without pushing too hard, and take care not to dislodge the painted dots. Refrigerate 5–10 minutes to set. If the edges are thin, carefully brush more chocolate around the edges and refrigerate for 5 more minutes. Carefully unmold. Set aside 6 of the shells for the tops. Melt the edges of 6 of the shells that will be the bottoms. Fill these cocoa bomb shells with: 1 tablespoon hot cocoa mix, a cookie-dough flavored marshmallow and/or a few mini marshmallows, and a handful of mini chocolate chips and/or cookie dough bites. Melt the edges of the leftover shells and attach the tops to bottoms. Let set.

To Make: Place a hot cocoa bomb in the bottom of a mug. Add approximately 10 ounces of very hot milk and stir well. Microwave for an extra 20 seconds to thoroughly combine ingredients and stir well again. Enjoy the fact that you don't have to wash 3 cookie sheets!

Regal Chocolate Raspberry Cocoa Bombs

This hot cocoa bomb is a crown jewel fit for a reigning monarch. The rich, deep chocolate melds with the freshness of raspberry to create a luscious and royal treat. A dark red luster powder and a small square of pure edible gold add to the royal treatment. Freeze-dried raspberries infuse their freshness into the chocolate the second they hit the hot liquid. The tartness pairs nicely with the cocoa. Raspberry oil in the chocolate shell is not necessary but creates a smooth, rich flavor. When decorating with gold leaf, make sure you've got edible gold leaf and not artist-grade, and work very gently with a brush or a pair of clean, food-only tweezers to gently place the gold on top of the freeze-dried raspberry. Try to make sure you don't breathe on it or have any air flow as you're working on this, as the gold leaf will break off or flatten to the raspberry with the slightest whisper of air.

MAKES 6 REGULAR COCOA BOMBS

Red luster powder
12 ounces milk chocolate candy melts *or* milk chocolate, tempered
½ teaspoon raspberry flavor oil, or to taste
1 recipe batch hot cocoa mix (page 40) *or* store-bought mix
Freeze-dried raspberries
Edible gold leaf, for decorating
½ cup milk chocolate candy melts *or* milk chocolate, tempered, for decorating

To Make: Place a hot cocoa bomb in the bottom of a mug. Add 10 ounces of very hot milk and stir well. Reheat in the microwave for approximately 20 seconds to thoroughly heat and stir well again for best taste. Put your slippered feet up on a velvet cushion and sip a gold-tinged royal beverage.

Use a dry, fluffy brush to lightly dust the interior of 12 half-sphere molds with red luster powder, reserving some luster powder to put inside the bombs. Melt the chocolate and thoroughly stir in the flavoring to taste. Pour 1–2 tablespoons melted chocolate into each mold and use a brush or the back of a spoon to make sure the chocolate fills in all of the mold and up the edges. Refrigerate 5 minutes to set. If the edges are thin, carefully brush more chocolate around the edges and refrigerate for 5 more minutes. Carefully unmold. Set aside 6 of the shells for the tops. Melt the edges of 6 of the shells that will be the bottoms. Fill these cocoa bomb shells with: 1 tablespoon hot cocoa mix, a pinch of red luster powder, and a handful of freeze-dried raspberries. Melt the edges of the leftover shells and attach the tops to bottoms. Let set. Meanwhile, spread the extra 2 ounces of chocolate on a sheet of parchment or wax paper in about ¼ inch thickness. Place in the refrigerator for a few minutes until solid. To decorate, break the flat chocolate into shards. Heat the pan or plate you used to melt the edges of the cocoa bombs again to melt the edges of a shard of chocolate for each cocoa bomb, and place it on top slightly off-center at a slight angle and hold it in place until it stands on its own. Then place a beautiful full freeze-dried raspberry in front of each chocolate shard. If the raspberry feels unsteady, use a brush with a bit of melted chocolate or a dab of edible glue to attach it to the shell. Very, very gently use a brush to apply a small square of edible gold leaf to the raspberry on top of each cocoa bomb.

Mom's Favorite Malt Balls Cocoa Bombs

This cocoa bomb is a special request from my mother-in-law, and my own mom loves malt balls, too. Of course, malt balls are inspired by a chocolate malt, so when adding these flavors to a hot cup of milk, it tastes like a delicious hot chocolate malted. If you've ever had Horlicks from England, which is a hot malted milk drink that also comes in chocolate flavor, it's similar to that. A nightly hot malted cocoa might become your new favorite tradition. You'll make mom proud!

MAKES 6 REGULAR COCOA BOMBS

12 ounces milk chocolate candy melts *or* milk chocolate, tempered
1 recipe batch hot cocoa mix (page 40) *or* ½ cup store-bought mix
½ cup malted milk powder
Mini chocolate chips
Malted milk chocolate balls, crushed, plus extra for decorating
Edible glue *or* melted chocolate, for decorating

Melt the chocolate and pour 1–2 tablespoons of the melted chocolate into each mold. Use a brush or the back of a spoon to make sure the chocolate fills in all of the mold and up the edges. Refrigerate 5 minutes to set. If the edges are thin, carefully brush more chocolate around the edges and refrigerate for 5 more minutes. Carefully unmold. Set aside 6 of the shells for the tops. Melt the edges of 6 of the shells that will be the bottoms. Fill these cocoa bomb shells with: 1 tablespoon hot cocoa mix, 1 tablespoon malted milk powder (or to taste), and a few crushed malted milk balls. Melt the edges of the leftover shells and attach. Let set. To decorate, spread a bit of edible glue or melted chocolate on the top of each bomb. Sprinkle a pinch of malted milk powder and add a few crushed pieces of malted milk chocolate balls.

To Make: Place a hot cocoa bomb in the bottom of a mug. Add 10 ounces of very hot milk and stir well. Reheat in the microwave for approximately 20 seconds to thoroughly heat and stir well again for best taste. Bring to your unsuspecting mother while she's relaxing in her favorite chair and get ready to be called her favorite child.

Chocolate Cheesecake Cocoa Bombs

This recipe is worth making just to lick the spoon after you flavor the chocolate! That lusciously creamy, chocolate dreamy-ness is unbelievable. When you order chocolate cheesecake at a gourmet restaurant, they are always topped with tiny chocolate chips, so add the smallest chocolate chips you can to this cocoa bomb. I also ordered freeze-dried cheesecake to really take this cocoa bomb over the edge. Use a deep, dark rich cocoa mix if you want a truly luxurious experience. Perhaps the best part about this recipe is that the cocoa bomb, without a doubt, has fewer calories than a piece of famous-brand cheesecake you might order at a restaurant.

MAKES 6 REGULAR COCOA BOMBS

12 ounces milk chocolate candy melts *or* milk chocolate, tempered
½–1 teaspoon cheesecake flavoring oil, to taste
1 recipe batch hot cocoa mix (page 40) *or* ½ cup store-bought mix
Mini chocolate chips
2 ounces freeze-dried cheesecake pieces, plus extra for decorating, optional
Edible glue *or* extra melted chocolate, for decorating

Melt the chocolate and thoroughly stir in the flavoring oil to taste. Pour 1–2 tablespoons melted chocolate into each mold. Use a brush or the back of a spoon to make sure the chocolate fills in all of the mold and up the edges. Refrigerate 5 minutes to set. If the edges are thin, carefully brush more chocolate around the edges and refrigerate for 5 more minutes. Carefully unmold. Set aside 6 of the shells for the tops. Melt the edges of 6 of the shells that will be the bottoms. Fill these cocoa bomb shells with: 1 tablespoon hot cocoa mix, several mini chocolate chips, and a piece or two of freeze-dried cheesecake, if you have it. Melt the edges of the leftover shells and attach. Let set. If desired, use a bit of edible glue or extra chocolate to top each bomb with an extra piece of freeze-dried cheesecake.

> **To Make:** Place a hot cocoa bomb in the bottom of a mug (hopefully a fancy one with a gold bottom!). Add 10 ounces of very hot milk and stir well. Feel like you're in a fancy café drinking a way-too-expensive hot cocoa that's totally worth every penny. Feel even better knowing you made these yourself.

Churro Cocoa Bombs

This sweet Spanish fried dough coated in cinnamon-sugar is a treat that is often eaten dipped in hot chocolate, so this pair is a match made in heaven (well, Spain, but it's close). They also look so charming and appealing with a swirl of cinnamon sugar. I've added hot cocoa mix here to give that idea of a churro dipped in hot chocolate, but feel free to use white cocoa as well for a more thoroughly cinnamon cocoa. Be careful with the cinnamon flavoring oil; it's very strong, so start with just a drop or two. The vanilla flavoring oil balances it nicely and gives the effect of the pastry dough churro. If you can find churros, fresh or frozen, I highly recommend dipping them in this hot chocolate. In Spain, and in my house, this churro-hot chocolate combination is frequently enjoyed for breakfast, an after-school snack, or an afternoon pick-me-up.

MAKES 6 REGULAR COCOA BOMBS

12 ounces white candy melts *or* white chocolate, tempered
¼–½ teaspoon vanilla flavoring oil
⅛ teaspoon cinnamon flavoring oil
1 recipe batch hot cocoa mix (page 40) *or* ½ cup store-bought mix
½ cup mini dehydrated marshmallows
Churro-flavored marshmallows
½ cup sugar, for decoration
1 teaspoon cinnamon, for decoration
Edible glue *or* melted white chocolate, for decoration

Melt the chocolate and thoroughly stir in the flavoring oils to taste. Pour 1–2 tablespoons melted chocolate into each mold. Use a brush or the back of a spoon to make sure the chocolate fills in all of the mold and up the edges. Refrigerate 5 minutes to set. If the edges are thin, carefully brush more chocolate around the edges and refrigerate for 5 more minutes. Carefully unmold. Set aside 6 of the shells for the tops. Melt the edges of 6 of the shells that will be the bottoms. Fill these cocoa bomb shells with: 1 tablespoon hot cocoa mix, a handful of mini marshmallows, and one or two churro-flavored marshmallows. Melt the edges of the leftover shells and attach. Let set. Mix the extra sugar and cinnamon in a small bowl. Make circular swirls of edible glue or melted but cool white chocolate on the tops of the cocoa bombs. Carefully dip the cocoa bomb tops in the cinnamon-sugar mix or carefully pour it on top to adhere to the glue or melted chocolate. Let set.

To Make: Place a hot cocoa bomb in the bottom of a mug. Add 10 ounces of very hot milk and stir well. If you're feeling like you need even more pep in your step, add some instant coffee.

Dulce de Leche Cocoa Bombs

Dulce de leche is the candy of milk or the "caramel of milk," in a loose translation, and is a standard Argentinian sweet. It differs from the caramel you're probably most familiar with, which is simply caramelized sugar. Dulce de leche is created by caramelizing the sugars in milk, resulting in a thick, creamy, milk-based caramel. Unfortunately, this milk base means it needs to be refrigerated. The dulce de leche flavoring oil in this recipe allows you to really nail that flavor without requiring the refrigeration, but if you don't want to purchase an extra flavor oil, you can go without. The mini caramels melted into the hot milk will be enough to create a rich and delicious drink. I've used white cocoa mix here instead of regular, to fully enhance the creaminess. Feel free to use regular hot cocoa mix instead for a cup of chocolate-caramel goodness. If you've been working on tempering chocolate, or want to try, this recipe is a great one to try tempering with Callenbaut's "gold" caramel couverture tablets. They may be a bit tricky, but they'll create a beautiful, golden shell with light caramel flavor.

MAKES 6 REGULAR COCOA BOMBS

12 ounces white candy melts *or* white chocolate, tempered, divided
Caramel oil-based candy/food coloring oil
½–1 teaspoon dulce de leche flavoring oil, to taste
1 recipe batch white cocoa mix (page 41) *or* ½ cup store-bought mix
Mini caramel bits
½ cup mini dehydrated marshmallows
Edible gold glitter, for decorating
A small amount of vegetable oil, for decorating

Melt the chocolate and thoroughly stir in the flavoring oils to taste. Add a few drops of caramel food coloring and barely stir. Don't worry, it will swirl as you pour! Pour 1–2 tablespoons melted chocolate into each mold. Use a brush or the back of a spoon to make sure the chocolate fills in all of the mold and up the edges. Refrigerate 5–10 minutes to set. If the edges are thin, carefully brush more chocolate around the edges and refrigerate for 5 more minutes. Carefully unmold. Set aside 6 of the shells for the tops. Melt the edges of 6 of the shells that will be the bottoms. Fill these cocoa bomb shells with: 1 tablespoon white cocoa mix, a few caramel bits, and a handful of mini marshmallows. Melt the edges of the leftover shells and attach. Let set. Mix about a teaspoon of gold edible glitter with a few drops of vegetable oil to create a gold "paint." Use a thin, clean, dry, food-only brush to follow some of the swirl lines with the gold paint and add dimension. Let dry.

> **To Make:** Admire your marbled, gilded dulce de leche geode-like cocoa bomb. Place in the bottom of a mug. Add 10 ounces of very hot milk and stir well.

Parisienne *Haut Chocolat* Cocoa Bombs

There's a reason most people go to Paris in the spring. It rains in the fall, and while rain in Paris might be romantic in a movie, it's not so much fun in reality when your shoes get soaked and the Eiffel Tower is just a blur of lights instead of a shining beacon of all things Parisian. But the good thing about Paris in the fall, and in the rain? Cafés. Espresso. Croissants. Pastries. Macarons. Haut Chocolat. What a great excuse to duck into every other café for a pick-me-up. Parisian hot chocolate, or haut chocolat, is thick sipping chocolate, served in a very small cup and often accompanied with a croissant for dipping. I added some of my favorite Paris-inspired flavors—bergamot, rose, and fresh lavender—to create a wonderful Parisienne, feminine cocoa that captures the sigh of relief one finds from removing a sodden coat and seeking refuge in a warm café.

MAKES 6 REGULAR COCOA BOMBS

10–12 ounces dark chocolate candy melts *or* dark chocolate, tempered
½–1 teaspoon bergamot flavoring oil, to taste
¼ teaspoon rose flavoring oil, to taste
1 recipe batch hot cocoa mix (page 40) *or* ½ cup store-bought mix
½ cup mini dehydrated marshmallows
Fresh dried culinary lavender, plus extra for decorating
Purple powdered food coloring, optional
Edible glue or extra chocolate, for decorating

Melt the chocolate and thoroughly stir in the flavoring oils to taste. Pour 1–2 tablespoons melted chocolate into each mold. Use a brush or the back of a spoon to make sure the chocolate fills in all of the mold and up the edges. Refrigerate 5–10 minutes to set. If the edges are thin, carefully brush more chocolate around the edges and refrigerate for 5 more minutes. Carefully unmold. Set aside 6 of the shells for the tops. Melt the edges of 6 of the shells that will be the bottoms. Fill these cocoa bomb shells with: 1 tablespoon hot cocoa mix, a handful of mini marshmallows, a pinch of lavender, and a pinch of purple food coloring powder, if desired. Melt the edges of the leftover shells and attach. Let set. Use a crème brûlée torch to barely heat the top of one cocoa bomb, or use a bit of edible glue or melted chocolate, and quickly sprinkle with extra lavender and/or rose petals so they adhere. Repeat for all cocoa bombs.

To Make: Place in the bottom of a mug. Add 6–8 ounces of very hot milk and stir well. Lose yourself in the unique flavors and aromas of this slightly-purple, floral hot cocoa.

Bacon-Chocolate Cocoa Bombs

This cocoa bomb recipe, especially when made in a heart mold, is the absolute perfect gift for the bacon-loving man (or anyone!) in your life. The smokiness of bacon oil brings a unique taste to the milk chocolate, and the inherent bacon-saltiness really combines the two. Use regular hot cocoa mix or a bacon-maple mix, if you can find one, for an extra dose of bacon. Shelf-stable bacon-flavored pieces give a hint at the flavor, but once the hot milk hits the cocoa bomb and releases that classic bacon scent, there will be no mistaking this unique cocoa bomb's personality. It pairs well with a hearty winter breakfast, or as a warming drink after a long hard morning of shoveling snow. Be sure to taste the chocolate as you add the flavoring; different bacon-flavored oils will have different levels of saltiness and smokiness, so adjust to your tastes.

MAKES 6 REGULAR COCOA BOMBS

12 ounces milk chocolate candy melts *or* milk chocolate, tempered
½–1 teaspoon bacon flavoring oil, to taste
1 recipe batch hot cocoa mix (page 40) *or* ½ cup store-bought mix
½ cup mini dehydrated marshmallows
Shelf-stable bacon-flavored pieces, for decorating
Edible glue *or* extra chocolate, for decorating

Melt the chocolate and thoroughly stir in the flavoring oil to taste. Pour 1–2 tablespoons melted chocolate into each mold. Use a brush or the back of a spoon to make sure the chocolate fills in all of the mold and up the edges. Refrigerate 5–10 minutes to set. If the edges are thin, carefully brush more chocolate around the edges and refrigerate for 5 more minutes. Carefully unmold. Set aside 6 of the shells for the tops. Melt the edges of 6 of the shells that will be the bottoms. Fill these cocoa bomb shells with: 1 tablespoon hot cocoa mix and a handful of mini marshmallows. Melt the edges of the leftover shells and attach. Let set. Use a crème brûlée torch to barely heat the top of one cocoa bomb, or a bit of edible glue or melted chocolate, and quickly sprinkle with the bacon pieces so they adhere. Repeat for all cocoa bombs.

To Make: Place in the bottom of a mug. Add 8–10 ounces of very hot milk and stir well. Serve with a "stir stick" of a crisp strip of bacon or a bacon-maple lollipop, as shown in the picture.

Vanilla Malt White Chocolate Cocoa Bombs

My husband's grandfather owned a pharmacy on Main St. in a quaint Chicago suburb. I wish I had seen it, complete with an old-fashioned soda fountain! We are lucky enough to have a few vintage crates from the soda fountain, and that the bones of it are still there as a café now. We visit whenever we can. This vanilla malt always makes me think of that era: shining chrome, sharing malts with a sweetheart, stealing gumballs (wait, not that last one). It makes me want to slip on some saddle shoes and pop a dime in the jukebox . . . and this vanilla malt hot cocoa will make you feel the same way!

MAKES 6 REGULAR COCOA BOMBS

12 ounces white candy melts *or* white chocolate, tempered
1 teaspoon vanilla flavoring oil, to taste
1 recipe batch white cocoa mix (page 41) *or* ½ cup store-bought mix
½ cup mini dehydrated marshmallows
½ cup malted milk powder

Melt the chocolate and thoroughly stir in the flavoring oil to taste. Pour 1–2 tablespoons melted chocolate into each mold. Use a brush or the back of a spoon to make sure the chocolate fills in all of the mold and up the edges. Refrigerate 5 minutes to set. If the edges are thin, carefully brush more chocolate around the edges and refrigerate for 5 more minutes. Carefully unmold. Set aside 6 of the shells for the tops. Melt the edges of 6 of the shells that will be the bottoms. Fill these cocoa bomb shells with: 1 tablespoon white cocoa mix, a handful of mini marshmallows, and 1 tablespoon malted milk powder (or to taste). Melt the edges of the leftover shells and attach tops to bottoms. Let set.

To Make: Place a hot cocoa bomb in the bottom of a mug. Add 8–10 ounces of very hot milk and stir well. Add two straws and share with someone you have a crush on!

Honey-Lovin' Cocoa Bombs

The moment hot milk hits this honey-infused cocoa bomb, the air fills with a warm, comforting, cozy aroma. Dark chocolate pairs well with honey, and adding honey flavor oil steps it up a notch (but is not necessary). Honey crystals instead of sugar in the hot cocoa mix add another layer of honey flavor. If you haven't added honey flavoring to the dark chocolate shells, I recommend serving these with a honey-filled stick to swirl in. Make sure you grab your honey sticks at a farmers market or local store, because not only do we need to support our local beekeepers, most cheap honey is imported and flavorless. The flowers on top are a cute little reminder to plant honey-bee-friendly plants in your garden. Honey bees love old-fashioned flowers, especially apple tree blossoms, bee balm, echinacea, peonies, poppies, marigolds, and cornflowers. This sweet drink pairs well with a crunchy, spicy treat. Swedish ginger thins are my favorite. A little dip, a little dunk . . . the honey, chocolate, and ginger are a perfect combination.

MAKES 6 REGULAR COCOA BOMBS

10 ounces dark chocolate candy melts *or* dark chocolate, tempered
½ teaspoon honey flavor oil, if desired
½ cup cocoa powder
½ cup honey crystals
½ teaspoon salt
Sugar bees, optional
Edible glue or a tiny bit of vegetable oil
Honey crystals, for decoration
Edible dried spring flowers, such as marigold, calendula, cornflower, or rose

Melt the chocolate and thoroughly stir in the flavoring to taste. Pour 1–2 tablespoons melted chocolate into each mold and use a brush or the back of a spoon to make sure the chocolate fills in all of the mold and up the edges. Refrigerate 5 minutes to set. If the edges are thin, carefully brush more chocolate around the edges and refrigerate for 5 more minutes. Carefully unmold. Set aside 6 of the shells for the tops. Melt the edges of 6 of the shells that will be the bottoms. Fill these cocoa bomb shells with: 1 tablespoon cocoa, 1 tablespoon honey crystals, a few grains of salt, and a sugar honey bee if desired. Melt the edges of the leftover shells and attach tops to bottoms. Let set. To decorate, use a paintbrush to swirl vegetable oil or edible glue on top, or quickly heat with a crème brûlée torch. Sprinkle honey crystals in the center and gently push edible dried flowers around the edges.

To Make: Place a hot cocoa bomb in the bottom of a mug. Add 8–10 ounces of very hot milk and stir well. Reheat in the microwave for approximately 20 seconds to thoroughly heat and stir well again for best taste. Grab a seed catalog and plan your bee-friendly garden while dreaming of spring!

Mocha and French Vanilla Creamer Cocoa Bombs

These mini, 2-inch bombs are such fun gifts for any coffee-drinker in your life. A jar with a mix of them is perfect; the mocha bomb has hot cocoa mix and a bit of cream, and the white chocolate one has just French vanilla creamer. I suggest adding only 1 teaspoon of creamer to the mocha bomb and 1 tablespoon to the white chocolate bombs, but this is how I like my coffee. Feel free to adjust the amounts to your liking! Of course, you can use this as a base recipe to make all sorts of creamer-inspired cocoa bombs, such as hazelnut or plain, or seasonal offerings such as sugar cookie or pumpkin pie creamer. I don't decorate these, as I love the mix of colors and the shiny smaller size, but feel free to decorate if desired. I certainly wouldn't say no to sprinkles and marshmallows in coffee!

MAKES 12 MINI 2-INCH COCOA BOMBS (6 OF EACH FLAVOR)

8 ounces milk chocolate candy melts *or* milk chocolate, tempered
8 ounces white candy melts *or* white chocolate, tempered
½ cup hot cocoa mix, homemade (page 40) or store-bought
¾ cup French vanilla dried coffee creamer, divided

To Make: Place a hot cocoa bomb in the bottom of a mug. Add 8–10 ounces of very hot **coffee** and stir well. Reheat in the microwave for approximately 20 seconds to thoroughly heat and stir well again for best taste. These make a great gift with a bag of locally-roasted coffee, especially for new neighbors, if you can bear to give any away.

Melt the milk chocolate and pour 1 tablespoon melted chocolate into each mold. Use a brush or the back of a spoon to make sure the chocolate fills in all of the mold and up the edges. Refrigerate 5 minutes to set. If the edges are thin, carefully brush more chocolate around the edges and refrigerate for 5 more minutes. Carefully unmold. Set aside 6 of the shells for the tops. Melt the edges of 6 of the shells that will be the bottoms. Fill these cocoa bomb shells with: 1 tablespoon cocoa and 1 teaspoon French vanilla dried creamer. Melt the edges of the leftover shells and attach. Let set.

Melt the white chocolate and and pour 1 tablespoon melted chocolate into each mold. Use a brush or the back of a spoon to make sure the chocolate fills in all of the mold and up the edges. Refrigerate 5 minutes to set. If the edges are thin, carefully brush more chocolate around the edges and refrigerate for 5 more minutes. Carefully unmold. Set aside 6 of the shells for the tops. Melt the edges of 6 of the shells that will be the bottoms. Fill these cocoa bomb shells with: 1 tablespoon French vanilla dried creamer. Melt the edges of the leftover shells and attach tops to bottoms. Let set.

Blue New Galaxy Cocoa Bombs

These galaxy cocoa bombs are fascinating . . . are they miniature galaxies in and of themselves, or are they "moon rocks" from a planet not yet discovered, or moons themselves from another dimension? It's up to your imagination! I love the mix of blue and black colorings, and a Milky-Way style streak of black edible glitter and a tail of blue and silver rocks and sprinkles . . . all melting into a fantastically blue sweet drink. This is an impressive cocoa bomb for sure! The flavoring, or lack thereof, is up to you. What can you imagine a far-away galaxy tasting like? Mine tastes like blueberry marshmallows, but maybe yours doesn't. A rock candy stir stick is fun, too!

MAKES 6 REGULAR COCOA BOMBS

12 ounces white candy melts *or* white chocolate, tempered
½ teaspoon blueberry flavor oil, or to taste
1 teaspoon marshmallow or whipped cream flavor oil, to taste
Black, light blue, dark blue, and purple oil-based food coloring
1 recipe batch white cocoa mix (page 41) *or* ½ cup store-bought hot cocoa mix
Blue powdered food coloring (or purple or black)
1 cup dehydrated mini marshmallows
Black edible glitter
Galaxy-inspired sprinkles, such as silver "moon rocks" and stars
Extra melted chocolate, edible glue, or a small amount of coconut oil for decorating

Melt the chocolate and thoroughly stir in the flavoring oils to taste. Add a few drops of each color of food coloring to the top of the chocolate. Stir only once or twice; it will marble as you pour. Pour 1–2 tablespoons melted chocolate into each mold and use a brush or back of a spoon to make sure the chocolate fills in all of the mold and up the edges. Refrigerate 5 minutes to set. If the edges are thin, carefully brush more chocolate around the edges and refrigerate for 5 more minutes. Carefully unmold. Set aside 6 of the shells for the tops. Melt the edges of 6 of the shells that will be the bottoms. Fill these cocoa bomb shells with: 1 tablespoon white cocoa mix, a liberal handful of the dehydrated mini marshmallows, a pinch of blue powdered food coloring, and any sprinkles you'd like inside. Melt the edges of the leftover shells and attach tops to bottoms. Let set.

To decorate, use a clean dry brush to lightly paint a 1-inch streak down the middle of one bomb in cool melted chocolate or a thin coating of edible glue or coconut oil. If using melted chocolate, make sure it isn't so hot that it will melt the cocoa bomb, and work quickly. Cover with black edible glitter and add sprinkles. Let set. Repeat for all cocoa bombs.

To Make: Place a hot cocoa bomb in the bottom of a mug. Add 10 ounces of very hot milk and stir well. If you happen to have any astronaut ice cream around from your last museum visit, add it to your cocoa bombs for a truly out-of-this-world taste experience.

Toasted Coconut Cocoa Bombs

Toasted coconut adds a nice nutty flavor and texture to this cocoa bomb, which pairs so nicely with a dark chocolate shell. For the toasted coconut, use unsweetened shredded coconut if you can find it (check the natural foods section). It toasts up much more nicely and gets a satisfying nutty flavor. Sweetened flaked coconut, usually in the baking aisle, is sticky and tricky to toast without burning. Similarly, larger flakes or fresh coconut are also hard to toast without burning. However, since it is not sweetened, you may find yourself wanting to add a few more marshmallows or a sprinkle of coconut sugar to the cocoa mix. It is really fun to fully cover these bombs in toasted coconut to resemble the shaggy exterior of a fresh coconut. Keep in mind, this will add texture to the cocoa, much like pulp in orange juice. Again, much like orange juice, some people love this and others aren't fans.

10 ounces dark chocolate candy melts *or* dark chocolate, tempered and ready to use
½ teaspoon toasted coconut flavor oil, or to taste
1 recipe batch hot cocoa mix (page 40) *or* ½ cup store-bought hot cocoa mix
12 toasted coconut marshmallows
1 cup dehydrated mini marshmallows
Mini chocolate-dipped coconut patties
2 cups unsweetened shredded coconut
Extra melted chocolate, edible glue, or a small amount of baking oil for decorating

To Make: Place a hot cocoa bomb in the bottom of a mug. Add 8–10 ounces of very hot milk and stir well. If you're not into the texture of the coconut, you can allow it to steep for a few minutes to infuse the flavor into the hot milk and then strain it out. Dig around in your kitchen junk drawer and see if you can find a mini drink umbrella to complete the tropical vibe.

Melt the chocolate and thoroughly stir in the flavoring oil to taste. Pour 1–2 tablespoons melted chocolate into each mold and use a brush or back of a spoon to make sure the chocolate fills in all of the mold and up the edges. Refrigerate 5 minutes to set. If the edges are thin, carefully brush more chocolate around the edges and refrigerate for 5 more minutes. Carefully unmold. Set aside 6 of the shells for the tops. Melt the edges of 6 of the shells that will be the bottoms. Fill these cocoa bomb shells with: 1 tablespoon cocoa mix, 2 toasted coconut marshmallows, a mini chocolate-dipped coconut patty, and a handful of dehydrated mini marshmallows. Melt the edges of the leftover shells and attach. Let set.

Preheat the oven to 350°F. Line a baking sheet with parchment paper or a silicone baking sheet. Spread the 2 cups of shredded coconut in a single layer. Toast for approximately 30 minutes, turning and tossing every 10 minutes. Look for a nice golden color and a great smell.

To decorate, use a clean dry brush to lightly coat one bomb in cool melted chocolate or a thin coating of edible glue or baking oil. If using melted chocolate, make sure it isn't so hot that it will melt the cocoa bomb, and work quickly. Cover with toasted coconut and lightly pat into the adhesive. Let set. Repeat for all cocoa bombs.

Chocolate-Covered Blueberry Cocoa Bombs

Have you ever purchased a container of chocolate-covered blueberries? If so, you probably know how hard it is to stop eating them! There's just something about that perfectly sweet-tartness of blueberries that pairs perfectly with chocolate. Make sure you use freeze-dried blueberries here and not regular dried blueberries. Freeze-dried blueberries plump back to life when added to liquid. Unless they're already covered with chocolate, regular dried blueberries will get rock hard with time. Chocolate-covered blueberries will soften a bit in the hot milk, but they may still be on the hard side, so be careful not to choke on them. This drink is one that seems to require wearing a sweater with elbow patches and wool slippers in front of a fire and escaping into another world by reading a book while drinking this. Word of warning, though: When decorating these, be very careful with petal dust. Petal dust is powerful stuff and will get everywhere and may stain clothing. Use with care, or choose a less-color-saturated food coloring powder instead.

MAKES 6 REGULAR COCOA BOMBS

2 ounces royal blue candy melts *or* white chocolate, tempered, and colored deep blue

10–12 ounces milk or dark chocolate candy melts *or* milk or dark chocolate, tempered

1 teaspoon blueberry flavor oil, or to taste

1 recipe batch hot cocoa mix (page 40) *or* ½ cup store-bought hot cocoa mix

½ cup freeze-dried blueberries

Chocolate-covered dried blueberries, plus extra for decorating

2 ounces milk or dark chocolate, melted, for decorating

Blue petal dust, for decorating

Melt the chocolate and thoroughly stir in the flavoring oil to taste. Pour 1–2 tablespoons melted chocolate into each mold and use a brush or back of a spoon to make sure the chocolate fills in all of the mold and up the edges. Refrigerate 5 minutes to set. If the edges are thin, carefully brush more chocolate around the edges and refrigerate for 5 more minutes. Carefully unmold. Set aside 6 of the shells for the tops. Melt the edges of 6 of the shells that will be the bottoms. Fill these cocoa bomb shells with: 1 tablespoon cocoa mix, 1 tablespoon freeze-dried blueberries, and a few chocolate-covered blueberries. Melt the edges of the leftover shells and attach tops to bottoms. Let set. To decorate, dip the bottom of a chocolate-covered blueberry lightly in the melted chocolate and attach to the top of a cocoa bomb. Repeat for all cocoa bombs. Let set. Then, use a brush dipped in the petal dust to color the chocolate-covered blueberry toppers.

To Make: Place a hot cocoa bomb in the bottom of a mug. Add 8–10 ounces of very hot milk and stir well. Reheat in the microwave for approximately 20 seconds to thoroughly heat and stir well again for best taste. Put on your most pretentious sweater, and read your most pretentious book. Well done.

Gorgeous Glitter Cocoa Bombs

These cocoa bombs are inspired by glamour, beauty, and all things elegant. They're filled with white cocoa, a white chocolate truffle, and gold and red "accessories"—that is, glitter, sequins, and candy! Mixing luster powder with a bit of plain vodka or vegetable oil creates a metallic paint reminiscent of makeup, and red edible paint reminiscent of lipstick. Get creative when you're painting these, there's no right or wrong way to decorate them. These are fun for a girl's night in, a bridal shower, or a teen sleepover.

MAKES 6 REGULAR COCOA BOMBS

10–12 ounces white candy melts *or* white chocolate, tempered and ready to use
1 recipe batch white cocoa mix (page 41) *or* ½ cup store-bought mix
Small red round candies, such as Sixlets or Cherry Sours
White-chocolate truffles
Edible gold glitter
Edible red glitter
Metallic edible sequins
Edible red paint
Edible rose-gold luster dust
Edible gold luster dust
Vegetable oil or plain vodka

Melt the chocolate and pour 1–2 tablespoons melted chocolate into each mold. Use a brush or the back of a spoon to make sure the chocolate fills in all of the mold and up the edges. Refrigerate 5 minutes to set. If the edges are thin, carefully brush more chocolate around the edges and refrigerate for 5 more minutes. Carefully unmold. Set aside 6 of the shells for the tops. Melt the edges of 6 of the shells that will be the bottoms. Fill these cocoa bomb shells with: 1 tablespoon of cocoa mix, a few red candies, a white chocolate truffle, a dash of gold glitter, a dash of red glitter, and a sprinkle of edible sequins. Melt the edges of the leftover shells and attach. Let set. To decorate, mix a few drops of vegetable oil or plain vodka with a dash of rose gold luster dust in a very small bowl and stir with a food-safe brush. Do the same in a separate bowl with the gold luster dust. Decorate to your liking with the red edible paint, the rose gold paint, and the gold paint. Let dry.

To Make: Place a hot cocoa bomb in the bottom of a mug. Add 8–10 ounces of very hot milk and stir well. Reheat in the microwave for approximately 20 seconds to thoroughly heat and stir well again for best taste. Revel in the white chocolate, velvet, glittery glamour with a splash of lipstick red!

Gender Reveal Party Cocoa Bombs

Gender reveal parties are all the rage, so why not combine them with this cocoa bomb trend for a perfectly memorable announcement at a party? Give each parent a cup with a cocoa bomb, and have them pour hot milk over them at the same time to reveal the colored milk inside . . . pink or blue. You could also have them smash their cocoa bombs with a small mallet first to unveil the color inside. It's extra fun if each guest also has their own cocoa bomb, or is given one to take home. If they're enjoying their cocoa bomb there, be sure to give them mugs or heat-safe paper cups in the color of their gender guess, then see if the color of the inside matches their guess and cup! Decorating these with both pink and blue keeps the inside a secret. Find sprinkles, colored food powder, and glitter in pink or blue to fill these with. If you can find colored marshmallows, that's all the more fun! I found blue baby bottles and pink bows to be the main sprinkle candies in each choice, but feel free to use chicks, footprints, flowers, onesies, or really any sprinkles you can find that feel right for your couple. Remember this only makes 6 cocoa bombs, so if you're throwing a party you might need a few batches!

MAKES 6 REGULAR COCOA BOMBS

- 12 ounces white candy melts or white chocolate, tempered
- 1 recipe batch white hot cocoa (page 41) *or* ½ cup store-bought cocoa mix
- 1 teaspoon pink or blue powdered food coloring or colored edible glitter
- 1 teaspoon silver glitter, if using plain powdered food coloring
- Pink or blue sprinkles of several kinds
- 1 cup mini marshmallows
- 2 ounces pink candy melts *or* white chocolate, tempered and colored pink
- 2 ounces light blue candy melts *or* white chocolate, tempered and colored light blue
- Extra sprinkles, for decorating

Melt the chocolate and thoroughly stir in the flavoring oil to taste. Pour 1–2 tablespoons melted chocolate into each mold and use a brush or the back of a spoon to make sure the chocolate fills in all of the mold and up the edges. Refrigerate 5 minutes to set. If the edges are thin, carefully brush more chocolate around the edges and refrigerate for 5 more minutes. Carefully unmold. Set aside 6 of the shells for the tops. Melt the edges of 6 of the shells that will be the bottoms. Fill these cocoa bomb shells with: 1 tablespoon cocoa mix, a pinch of the food coloring powder, and a pinch of glitter, along with plenty of sprinkles and mini marshmallows. Melt the edges of the other six cocoa bomb shells and attach the tops to the bottoms. Let set. Melt the 2 ounces of pink chocolate and add to a piping bag with a very fine tip or a plastic bag and snip the corner to create a very small opening. Pipe lines across one direction. Repeat with the blue chocolate and pipe lines the opposite direction. Decorate with pink and blue sprinkles, if desired.

To Make: Place a hot cocoa bomb in the bottom of a mug. Add 10 ounces of very hot milk, stir well. Celebrate the coming addition of a wonderful new life to this wonderful world!

Confetti Fun Sprinkle Cake Cocoa Bombs

Confetti, fun, sprinkles, cake, frosting . . . does it get any better than that? The edible "confetti" in this classic cake is actually slightly-melted sprinkles that create colorful slightly-melted surprises throughout the cake. The original confetti cake was created at the end of the 1980s or early 1990s, and quickly became a cultural phenomenon, so it holds a lot of nostalgic value for many Millenials. The fun continues with these sprinkle-encrusted and marshmallow-filled cocoa bombs. Unfortunately, when all of the rainbow colors mix, most kids will learn some sad day in art class, they make . . . brown. In an effort to alleviate that sadness, add a bit of purple food coloring powder. Cake batter flavoring adds classic cake flavor, while vanilla frosting inside brings that sweet frosting layer that most kids eat first anyway, so why not add two scoops? Don't be afraid to really load up on the sprinkles and mini marshmallows; with confetti fun, the more the merrier!

MAKES 6 REGULAR COCOA BOMBS

12 ounces white candy melts *or* white chocolate, tempered
½ teaspoon–1 teaspoon cake batter flavoring, to taste
1 cup vanilla frosting
1 cup rainbow sprinkles
1–2 cups mini marshmallows
Decorations, optional

Tip: To add a birthday candle to the top, use a flame to melt the bottom of the candle and quickly and gently press it to the top of the cocoa bomb. Hold for 30 seconds to fully set.

Melt the chocolate and thoroughly stir in the flavoring oil to taste. Pour 1–2 tablespoons melted chocolate into each mold and use a brush or the back of a spoon to make sure the chocolate fills in all of the mold and up the edges. Refrigerate 5 minutes to set. If the edges are thin, carefully brush more chocolate around the edges and refrigerate for 5 more minutes. Carefully unmold. Set aside 6 of the shells for the tops. Melt the edges of 6 of the shells that will be the bottoms. Fill these cocoa bomb shells with 2 tablespoons vanilla frosting. Sprinkle each cocoa bomb half liberally with rainbow sprinkles and mini marshmallows. Melt the edges of the other six cocoa bomb shells and attach the tops to the bottoms. Let set. Decorate with melted candy melts, sprinkles, mini marshmallows, cookies, etc. as desired.

To Make: Place a hot cocoa bomb in the bottom of a mug. Add 10 ounces of very hot milk, stir well. Reheat in the microwave for approximately 20 seconds to thoroughly heat and melt the ingredients together. Stir well again. Get ready to say hurray for confetti cake in a cup!

Unicorn Party Cocoa Bombs

These unicorn cocoa bombs bring the party! They are so cheerful and inviting, and they are frolicking in a field of strawberry-flavored edible grass. No, seriously, that's what they are nestled in, and it's the stuff of dreams. They also taste like the stuff of dreams, with a strawberry and cotton candy combination that tastes like a rainbow. These might look difficult to make but don't be intimidated; I ordered the horns and ears from a maker on Etsy and I've even seen them in stores! Simply dip the beautiful decorations in white chocolate, attach, and refrigerate to set. If an ear slides out of place, just call that one sleepy and give her closed or winking eyes (like my little one in the back!). I think that just adds to the "party" effect! The eyes are drawn on carefully with an edible marker easily found in most candy- and cake-decorating stores. My unicorns dressed up extra-fancy for this party, wearing bows on their horns (attached with edible glue or melted white chocolate) and bright rosy rouge on their cheeks. Get creative with your decorating and plating, and make your unicorns as fancy as you'd like!

MAKES 6 REGULAR COCOA BOMBS

10–12 white candy melts *or* white chocolate, tempered
¼–½ teaspoon strawberry flavoring oil, or to taste
¼–½ teaspoon cotton candy flavoring oil, or to taste
2 ounces white chocolate, melted, for decorating
Unicorn horns and ears, for decorating
1 recipe batch white cocoa mix (page 41) *or* ½ cup store-bought mix
1 cup dehydrated mini marshmallows *or* rainbow twist marshmallows
Pink unicorn sprinkles (*omit* for younger children)
Gold unicorn horn sprinkles (*omit* for younger children)
Pink or any color of the rainbow powdered food coloring
Pink edible glitter
Bow and bauble sprinkles, for decorating
Black edible food-coloring marker, for decorating
Rose gold luster powder, for decorating
Edible strawberry grass, for serving
Colored sugar, for decorating

Melt the chocolate and add the flavoring oils to taste. Pour 1–2 tablespoons melted chocolate into each mold and use a brush or the back of a spoon to make sure the chocolate fills in all of the mold and up the edges. Refrigerate 5 minutes to set. If the edges are thin, carefully brush more chocolate around the edges and refrigerate for 5 more minutes. Carefully unmold. Set 6 aside for the bottoms and work on the tops first this time. Using the melted chocolate for decorating, carefully dip the bottom of the horn in chocolate and attach to the center of the top. Hold in place for 30 seconds. Quickly dip each ear in chocolate and attach to the base of the horn on each side, also holding each one in place for 30 seconds. Refrigerate for at least 5 minutes to allow them to fully attach and set.

Meanwhile, in the bottom of each of the other six shells, place 1 tablespoon white cocoa mix. Sprinkle each cocoa bomb half liberally with marshmallows. Add a few unicorn and unicorn horn sprinkles. Add ⅛ teaspoon food coloring powder of your choice to each cocoa bomb. Add a sprinkle of pink edible glitter to each cocoa bomb.

(Continued on next page)

Pull your unicorn heads out of the refrigerator and finish decorating them. Use a brush with more melted chocolate (you may need to re-melt it and that's fine!), or edible glue, and attach bows, colored sugar, and other decorations at the base of the horn as desired. Use an edible food marker to draw eyes. Use a small brush dipped in rose gold luster powder to give each unicorn rosy cheeks. Let these decorations fully set, especially if you used edible glue, in the refrigerator or at room temperature for at least 10 minutes to let everything fully adhere.

Once all of the decorations are fully set, melt the edges of the other six cocoa bomb shells and attach the tops to the bottoms. Let set. Fill a bowl or plate with lightly broken up edible grass, and let your unicorns frolic!

To Make: Place a hot cocoa bomb in the bottom of a mug. Add 8 ounces of very hot milk, stir well. Think about this: Did you know a group of unicorns is called a blessing? I vote to call it a "party" of unicorns.

Craft Party Cocoa Bombs

These cocoa bombs create a plain canvas for kids to go wild with the sprinkles, chocolate, and more. Be sure to put down a wipe-clean tablecloth or a big roll of butcher paper. I also recommend having the kids wear aprons. This will get messy. That's part of the fun! Be sure to have edible paints, food coloring markers, all sorts of sprinkles and sugars, and color and glitter powders. Use new paint brushes that have never been used for anything else and have been washed and thoroughly dried, or brushes specifically made for cake and candy work. Because the round bombs have a tendency to roll, melt under the heat of hands, etc., it's best to let kids decorate their halves separately in a shallow, wide bowl or container. Try to make sure the kids don't touch the chocolate shells too often or they will start to melt. Once the cocoa bomb halves they've created are dry/set, you can either have the kids fill them or have the grown-ups do that part if the kids have moved on to another activity. Be sure to only let grown-ups attach the halves safely. Then enjoy the second half of the party: hot cocoa drinking!

MAKES 6 REGULAR COCOA BOMBS

12 ounces bright white chocolate candy melts *or* white chocolate, tempered
Decorations in every color, shape and shimmer
Powdered food coloring
Glitter and shimmer powders
Extra melted (but not hot) chocolate in small containers for attaching decorations
Lots of food-only, clean and dry paint brushes
1 recipe batch white hot cocoa (page 41) *or* ½ cup store-bought mix
An abundance of mini marshmallows

Melt the chocolate. Pour 1–2 tablespoons melted chocolate into each mold and use a brush or the back of a spoon to make sure the chocolate fills in all of the mold and up the edges. Refrigerate 5 minutes to set. Carefully unmold.

Prepare by covering the table. Then create a decorating "station" for each child by placing their two halves in a wide, shallow container. Be sure to place a piece of tape on each child's container with their name so they don't get mixed up. Around the table, or in front of each child, however you prefer, place small bowls of sprinkles and powders, each with a spoon or brush, with extra brushes and spoons on the table. If you're going to have the children fill their cocoa bombs, have the cocoa mix and any interior additions ready as well. Give each child a dish of their own melted, but not hot, white chocolate and a brush to use as "glue" for the decorations.

Have the children wash their hands, put on their aprons, and start making a mess! Once everyone has thoroughly coated their cocoa bomb halves in color and sparkle, carefully remove their aprons (I suggest spraying with stain remover now!) and wash those sticky hands. Then let the cocoa bombs set in the refrigerator for at least 10 minutes.

(Continued on page 171)

Fill each cocoa bomb bottom with 1 tablespoon white cocoa mix and a handful of marshmallows. Have a grown-up heat the edges of the tops and attach them to the bottoms. Let set.

To Make: Place a hot cocoa bomb in the bottom of a mug. Add 10 ounces of very hot milk, stir well. Let cool before giving to kids! Remind yourself this was all worth it because you created a fantastic memory for your kids and their friends.

More Tips: *Don't forget to adjust the recipe as needed since this only makes 6 cocoa bombs and you're likely to have a few break and fall. Prevent tears ahead of time by making extra! *Feel free to have kids only decorate one half. *Make room in your refrigerator ahead of time to allow these to set. Chances are, kids will go heavy on the chocolate and they will need at least 10 minutes to set. *You can also send these home with kids as a party favor! Simply place them in clear bags and tie with a twist tie or ribbon. Don't forget to label them again so you make sure each kid gets their original cocoa bomb, and give instructions for using it. *You may want to warn children that all of the colors of sprinkles and decorations look pretty on the surface but are likely to create brown when melted together . . . cocoa brown, of course! *These are likely to be sweet enough without the cocoa mix after decorating, so feel free to simply fill them with marshmallows for the fun "exploding" effect without the extra sugar.

Childhood Favorites Cereal Milk Cocoa Bombs

Are you a cereal leftover-milk drinker or not? It's a hotly contested subject in my household, but no matter where you stand, cereal and milk is a childhood classic special breakfast. Bring those sugary, fruity flavors to hot cocoa with this fun bomb. It pairs perfectly well with a family living room sleepover, with everyone in pajamas, a fort made out of couch pillows and sheets, and an animated movie on the television (or on the wall, if you have a projector). I'm not saying I recommend this for breakfast, but it is technically cereal and milk, right?

MAKES 6 REGULAR COCOA BOMBS

Fruity cereal of your choice
10–12 ounces white candy melts *or* **white chocolate, tempered**
3–4 drops fruity stones cereal flavoring oil, or to taste
6–7 drops berry crunch cereal flavoring oil, or to taste
1 recipe batch white cocoa mix (page 41) *or* **½ cup store-bought mix**
1 cup dehydrated mini marshmallows

Crush up about ¼ cup of the fruity cereal of your choice and use the crumbs to dust the inside of 6 of the cocoa bomb molds. The crumbs will mostly go down to the bottom, but that's fine. Melt the white chocolate and thoroughly stir in the flavoring oils to taste. Pour 1–2 tablespoons melted chocolate into each mold and use a brush or the back of a spoon to make sure the chocolate fills in all of the mold and up the edges. Refrigerate 5 minutes to set. If the edges are thin, carefully brush more chocolate around the edges and refrigerate for 5 more minutes. Carefully unmold. Set 6 aside for the tops. In the bottom of each of the other six shells, place 1 tablespoon hot cocoa mix and plenty of mini marshmallows. Add a sprinkle of the fruity breakfast cereal of your choice. Melt the edges of the other six cocoa bomb shells and attach the tops to the bottoms. Let set. I like to keep these simple as far as decorations go, since they have the crushed cereal on the top already, that looks like it was just tipped out of the bowl.

To Make: Place a hot cocoa bomb in the bottom of a mug. Add 8–10 ounces of very hot milk, stir well. Don't forget to be kind and rewind the VHS. Oh wait, errr, turn off the smart TV before you fall asleep!

Cookies and Cream Cocoa Bombs

Who doesn't love a classic cookies and cream flavor? You might envision eating the cookies with a tall, cold glass of milk, but why not try them in a sturdy, hot mug of cocoa instead? The creaminess of the filling and the chocolatey-goodness of the cookie combine into a dreamy hot chocolate. If you can find cookies and cream-flavored candy melts, that makes this much easier! If not, you'll need to melt white candy melts or chocolate (tempered), and gently fold in thoroughly crushed chocolate wafer cookies. There are all sorts of cookies and cream flavored bits and pieces to add, so stroll down the candy and cookie aisles for inspiration. Feel free to load up on chocolate additions, too, or use a dark-chocolate hot cocoa mix to stand up to all of the "cream" in the milk. Extra marshmallows add to the creamy-filling flavor and texture.

MAKES 6 REGULAR COCOA BOMBS

- 10–12 ounces cookies and cream candy melts *or* white candy melts *or* white chocolate, tempered
- 6–8 chocolate wafer cookies, pulverized, if using plain candy melts or chocolate
- 1 recipe batch hot cocoa mix (page 40) *or* ½ cup store-bought cocoa mix
- 1 cup dehydrated mini marshmallows
- Cookies and cream drops/balls/ snacks
- Mini chocolate sandwich cookies

Melt the cookies and cream candy melts, or combine the wafer cookie crumbs with the melted white chocolate. Pour 1–2 tablespoons melted chocolate into each mold and use a brush or the back of a spoon to make sure the chocolate fills in all of the mold and up the edges. Refrigerate 5 minutes to set. If the edges are thin, carefully brush more chocolate around the edges and refrigerate for 5 more minutes. Carefully unmold. Set 6 aside for the tops. In the bottom of each of the other six shells, place 1 tablespoon hot cocoa mix. Sprinkle each cocoa bomb half liberally with mini marshmallows. Add a few cookies and cream drops and mini cookies to each bottom half. Melt the edges of the other six cocoa bomb shells and attach the tops to the bottoms. Let set. I like to keep these simple as far as decorations go, since I think the texture looks fantastic and inviting, particularly in a glass cookie jar to show them off. If you feel like adding more decorations, go for it!

To Make: Place a hot cocoa bomb in the bottom of a mug. Add 8 ounces of very hot milk, stir well. Reheat in the microwave for approximately 20 seconds to thoroughly heat and melt the ingredients together. Stir well again. Pat yourself on the back for drinking a delicious mug of cookies and cream cocoa instead of eating an entire package of cookies.

Cotton Candy Cocoa Bombs

Giant, fluffy clouds on a stick that you can hold, edible and so sweet they make your teeth hurt, are a child's delight! Normally reserved for summer events like the fair or amusement park, this cocoa bomb brings the flavors of cotton candy to winter. The swirls of pink cotton candy flavoring and the blue raspberry flavoring perfectly melt into white chocolate cocoa. Even if you opt not to use the flavorings, the colors of this drink evoke memories of walking around with a cone of cotton candy as big as your head, lights spinning overhead, feeling all of the big and small feelings a child does all at once. This cocoa bomb is sure to please all the child-like dreamers in your life.

MAKES 6 REGULAR COCOA BOMBS

4–6 ounces blue candy melts *or* white chocolate, tempered and colored blue

¼ teaspoon blue raspberry flavoring oil, or to taste

8–10 ounces pink candy melts *or* white chocolate, tempered and colored pink

½ teaspoon cotton candy flavoring oil, or to taste

1 recipe batch white hot cocoa mix (page 41) *or* ½ cup store-bought mix

½ cup mini dehydrated marshmallows

Pink and/or blue cotton candy, plus extra for decorating

A small amount of melted chocolate (white, pink, or blue) *or* edible glue, for decorating

Melt the blue chocolate and add the blue raspberry flavoring oil to taste. Use the back of a spoon to paint parts of each mold to create a swirl effect. Then melt the pink chocolate and add the cotton candy flavoring to taste. Fill the shells the rest of the way. Refrigerate 5 minutes to set. If the edges are thin, carefully brush more chocolate around the edges and refrigerate for 5 more minutes. Carefully unmold. Set aside 6 of the shells for the tops. Melt the edges of 6 of the cocoa bombs. Fill these cocoa bomb shells with: 1 tablespoon white hot cocoa mix, a handful of mini dehydrated marshmallows, and a small puff of cotton candy. Then melt the edge of the other halves of the cocoa bombs, one at a time, and stick them to the bottom halves. Let set. Use a small amount of melted chocolate or a dab of edible glue to attach a small piece of cotton candy to the top of each bomb.

To Make: Place a hot cocoa bomb in the bottom of a mug. Add 10 ounces of very hot milk, stir well. Microwave an additional 10–20 seconds to fully melt the ingredients and stir well. Hold your child's sticky hands in yours as you both drink this delightfully sweet drink, making memories of cotton candy dreams even in winter.

Back-to-School Vanilla Snack Cake Cocoa Bombs

Mmmm, when it comes to thinking about favorite childhood snacks, these vanilla snack cakes come to mind quickly. I remember I got in trouble one time, and was sent to my room without dinner. A little while later, my dad snuck up and gave me a peace offering of a single wrapped snack cake. So we all need a little snack cake to survive now and again! Small spongy cakes filled with a marshmallow-y, fluffy frosting, iced or plain, individually wrapped and tucked in a lunchbox as a surprise or thrown in a backpack for an after school treat, snack cakes are an American classic. To recreate the flavor in a hot cocoa bomb, add cake batter flavoring to the white chocolate shell for a bit of that sponge-cake taste. This cocoa bomb is unique in that it has a scoop of frosting and a scoop of marshmallow cream to recreate that specific filling and frosting flavor you remember. If you're feeling like going the extra mile, order some freeze-dried snack cake slices online (I got mine on Etsy) or add a few slices of fresh snack cake when serving. Lots of mini marshmallows is also key to achieving the overly-sweet flavor, so don't be ashamed to load it up!

MAKES 6 REGULAR COCOA BOMBS

12 ounces white candy melts *or* white chocolate, tempered
½–1 teaspoon cake batter flavoring oil, or to taste
½ cup vanilla whipped frosting
½ cup marshmallow fluff
Mini dehydrated marshmallows
A pinch of salt
Freeze-dried snack cake slices, optional

Melt the chocolate and thoroughly stir in the flavoring oil to taste. Pour 1–2 tablespoons melted chocolate into each mold and use a brush or the back of a spoon to make sure the chocolate fills in all of the mold and up the edges. Refrigerate 5 minutes to set. If the edges are thin, carefully brush more chocolate around the edges and refrigerate for 5 more minutes. Carefully unmold. Set aside 6 of the shells for the tops. Melt the edges of 6 of the cocoa bombs. Fill these cocoa bomb shells with: 1 tablespoon vanilla whipped frosting, 1 tablespoon marshmallow fluff, a few grains of salt, a handful of mini dehydrated marshmallows, and 2–3 slices freeze-dried snack cake. Then melt the edge of the other halves of the cocoa bombs, one at a time, and stick them to the bottom halves. Let set. Decorate as desired, with candy melts, sprinkles, mini marshmallows, and freeze-dried snack-cake pieces.

To Make: Place a hot cocoa bomb in the bottom of a mug. Add 10 ounces of very hot milk, stir well. Reheat in the microwave for approximately 20 seconds to thoroughly heat and melt the ingredients together. Stir well again. Enjoy a taste of childhood!

Pink Bubble Gum Heart Love Bombs

Well these are just the pinkest-prettiest love bombs I've ever seen! I guarantee if you serve these at any young girl's birthday party, "tea" party, or for a special afternoon treat they will ooh, ahh, and giggle with delight. My friend in her late-twenties went crazy over these, as did another friend's eight-year-old granddaughter. The fact that these taste exactly like bubble gum is really just a bonus. Load them up with pretty sprinkles, especially pink and white metallic pearls that look like bubbles. Those pieces of bubble gum on top? Shh, don't tell, but they are actually mini strawberry-flavored chewy candies that you can find in the candy aisle. They look like bubble gum and the strawberry taste really complements the bubble gum. Plus real bubble gum doesn't actually dissolve, so this is a perfectly neat little trick. The pink and white swirl really adds to the visual appeal of these, and is easy to achieve; simply swirl one color in with a spoon, and then spoon in the other! Starting with pink first creates a more-pink end result, which I prefer.

MAKES 6 HEART COCOA BOMBS

6 ounces pink candy melts *or* white chocolate, tempered and colored pink

8–10 ounces white candy melts *or* white chocolate, tempered

½–1 teaspoon bubble gum flavoring oil, or to taste

1 recipe batch white hot cocoa mix (page 41) *or* ½ cup store-bought mix

Mini dehydrated marshmallows

2 ounces white candy melts *or* white chocolate, tempered

Pink sprinkles galore

Mini dehydrated marshmallows, for decoration

Mini unwrapped strawberry fruit chew candies, for decoration

Melt the pink candy melts and add the flavoring oil to taste. Use a spoon to swirl the pink chocolate into the hearts in a random pattern, not filling in the entire bottom of the mold. Then fill the rest with the white chocolate, and use a brush or the back of a spoon to make sure the white chocolate fills in all of the mold and up the edges. These heart shapes are a bit trickier. Refrigerate 10 minutes to set. If the edges are thin, carefully brush more chocolate around the edges and refrigerate for 5 more minutes. Carefully unmold. Set aside 6 of the shells for the tops. Melt the edges of 6 of the shells that will be the bottoms. Fill these cocoa bomb shells with: 1 tablespoon white hot cocoa mix, 1 tablespoon marshmallows, and a few decorative sprinkles. Then melt the edges of the other halves of the cocoa bombs, one at a time, and stick them to the bottom halves. Let set. Melt the 2 ounces of candy melts or white chocolate, and add to a piping bag with a very fine tip or a plastic bag and snip the corner to create a very small opening. Pipe lines across one top corner of the hearts. Decorate as desired, with sprinkles, mini marshmallows, and strawberry fruit chew candies.

To Make: Place a hot cocoa bomb in the bottom of a mug. Add 10 ounces of very hot milk, stir well. Reheat in the microwave for approximately 20 seconds to thoroughly heat and melt the ingredients together. Stir well again. Try not to blow bubbles.

Mermaid Hot Cocoa Bombs

These cocoa bombs make a splash wherever they go! They draw you in with their mesmerizing turquoise powder, pearlescent gems, stunning starfish, and more. It's easy to create an entire beach scene with brown sugar as sand and an array of specialty sprinkles. Look for anything water-related or bubble-like, such as the small blue sugar pearls or the flat light pink shimmery sprinkles you can find if you look closely at the picture. I wasn't sure exactly what a mermaid flavor would be, so I went with a mix of raspberry, blueberry, and marshmallow that tastes pretty tropical to me, and kids are sure to love. The turquoise shimmer powder is non-negotiable for this fun drink, and you can absolutely add a bit of blue powdered food coloring if you want the milk to turn blue like ocean water. The shimmer powder adds a lovely light blue-green sheen to the finished drink.

MAKES 6 REGULAR COCOA BOMBS

Turquoise edible shimmer powder
12 ounces white candy melts *or* white chocolate, tempered
¼ teaspoon marshmallow flavoring oil, or to taste
¼ teaspoon raspberry flavoring oil, or to taste
¼ teaspoon blueberry flavoring oil, or to taste
1 recipe batch white hot cocoa mix (page 41) *or* ½ cup store-bought mix
½ cup mini dehydrated marshmallows
Brown sugar, for decoration
Turquoise edible shimmer powder, for decoration
Mini dehydrated marshmallows, for decoration
Pearl-like dragées/sprinkles, for decoration
All manner of blue, white, pink, purple, green, and yellow sprinkles, for decoration

Use a dry, fluffy brush to thoroughly cover half of the molds with the turquoise shimmer powder. Leave the other six molds plain. Melt the chocolate and thoroughly stir in the flavoring oils to taste. Pour 1–2 tablespoons melted chocolate into each mold and use a brush or the back of a spoon to make sure the chocolate fills in all of the mold and up the edges. Refrigerate 5 minutes to set. If the edges are thin, carefully brush more chocolate around the edges and refrigerate for 5 more minutes. Carefully unmold. Set aside 6 of the shells for the tops. Melt the edges of 6 of the shells that will be the bottoms. Fill these cocoa bomb shells with: 1 tablespoon white hot cocoa mix, 1 tablespoon marshmallows, and a few decorative sprinkles. Then melt the edges of the other halves of the cocoa bombs, one at a time, and stick them to the bottom halves. Let set. To serve, create a sand beach with the brown sugar and carefully place decorative sprinkles such as shells, candy rocks, shimmer sugar, pearl dragées, mermaid tails, etc. Place the cocoa bombs in the center.

To Make: Place a hot cocoa bomb in the bottom of a mug. Add 10 ounces of very hot milk, stir well. Reheat in the microwave for approximately 20 seconds to thoroughly heat and melt the ingredients together. Stir well again. Watch a tropical movie or documentary and dream of warm summer.

Treasure Chest Hot Cocoa Bombs

Adults and kids alike are fascinated by the idea of hidden treasure, submerged underwater for generations, discovered by an off-course diver, or discovered in a cliffside cave by adventurous children. It's not always fantasy . . . it actually happens, still to this day, which is what makes the stories so enticing. This cocoa bomb is filled with riches and treasures. I love to serve this one in a shallow bowl of brown-sugar "sand." Make sure to give the treasure-seeker the proper tool for opening a long-hidden chest: a small wooden mallet. Use the mallet to break the shell and explore all of the diamonds and rubies before adding them to the hot milk! Be very careful serving this to children, as some of the pieces of isomalt sugar can be large and choking hazards; these are best reserved to the side and eaten as hard candy on their own.

MAKES 6 REGULAR COCOA BOMBS

12 ounces milk chocolate candy melts *or* milk chocolate, tempered
1 recipe batch hot cocoa mix (page 40) *or* ½ cup store-bought mix
½ cup mini dehydrated marshmallows
Brown sugar, for decoration
Isomalt gems and diamonds
Gold, silver, and colored metallic dragées
Gold crown sprinkles
Melted very dark chocolate, or a black or brown edible marker

Pour 1–2 tablespoons melted chocolate into each mold and use a brush or the back of a spoon to make sure the chocolate fills in all of the mold and up the edges. Refrigerate 5 minutes to set. If the edges are thin, carefully brush more chocolate around the edges and refrigerate for 5 more minutes. Carefully unmold. Set aside 6 of the shells for the tops. Melt the edges of 6 of the shells that will be the bottoms. Fill these cocoa bomb shells with: 1 tablespoon white hot cocoa mix, 1 tablespoon marshmallows, and a handful of the decorative sprinkles/ edible items. Then melt the edge of the other halves of the cocoa bombs, one at a time, and stick them to the bottom halves. Let set. If desired, use melted dark chocolate or a black edible marker to create trunk-like details on the cocoa bomb or leave it secretive with no markings except an "X" to mark the spot.

To Make: Serve on a small plate or shallow bowl with a small food-only wooden mallet to break the treasure chest bomb open. Discover your treasures and set aside any that are large enough to cause a choking hazard. Then carefully transfer to a mug. Add 10 ounces very hot milk and stir well. Watch out for pirates!

Winter Wonderland Cocoa Bombs

Magic winter wonderlands, whether entered through a secret door at the back of an old wardrobe or breathed into life by a wintery princess, enchant us all, no matter what age. These winter wonderland cocoa bombs are inspired by those winter dreams where magical things happen and the doldrums of winter are suspended for a moment or two. Kids just think playing in the snow is inherently fun (especially putting back snow you've just shoveled) and relish any magical land, no matter the place or season. This cocoa bomb is for the kids, then, who will take great delight in coming in from a wintery outdoors to find an icy, sparkly, majestic winter treat in their cup. Add hot milk, and magic happens.

MAKES 6 REGULAR COCOA BOMBS

Light blue or turquoise edible shimmer powder
12 ounces white candy melts *or* white chocolate, tempered
¼–½ teaspoon marshmallow flavoring oil, or to taste
1 recipe batch white hot cocoa mix (page 41) *or* ½ cup store-bought mix
A few pinches of blue powdered food coloring
Mini dehydrated marshmallows
Blue petal powder, for decoration
2 ounces white candy melts or melted white chocolate, for decoration
A variety of white and blue sprinkles and sparkles, for decoration

Use a dry, fluffy brush to thoroughly cover half of the molds with the shimmer powder. Leave the other six molds plain. Melt the chocolate and thoroughly stir in the flavoring oil to taste. Pour 1–2 tablespoons melted chocolate into each mold and use a brush or the back of a spoon to make sure the chocolate fills in all of the mold and up the edges. Refrigerate 5 minutes to set. If the edges are thin, carefully brush more chocolate around the edges and refrigerate for 5 more minutes. Carefully unmold. Set aside 6 of the shells for the tops. Melt the edges of 6 of the shells that will be the bottoms. Fill these cocoa bomb shells with: 1 tablespoon white hot cocoa mix, a pinch of blue food coloring powder, 1 tablespoon marshmallows, and a few decorative sprinkles. Then melt the edge of the other halves of the cocoa bombs, one at a time, and stick them to the bottom halves. Let set. Use a brush dipped in the blue petal powder to make swirling motions all over the cocoa bombs, as if a winter princess had blown a storm into them. Melt the 2 ounces of candy melts or white chocolate, and add to a piping bag with a very fine tip or a plastic bag and snip to create a very small opening. Pipe lines across one top corner of the hearts. Decorate with sprinkles as desired.

To Make: Send the kids outside to play. Place a hot cocoa bomb in the bottom of a mug. Add 8–10 ounces of very hot milk and stir well. Drink your cup of cocoa in silence. Then invite the kids in and repeat, letting the cocoa cool to a much more kid-friendly temperature while they ooh and ahh.

Frosted Animal Circus Cookies Cocoa Bombs

These cookies have a special place in my heart. Not only are they nearly neon pink, white, and covered in frosting and sprinkles, they were one of the few treats my brother and I were only allowed to eat when we had a babysitter. This was a rare event, so they were always a super-sweet occasional treat. "Frosted animal cookies" flavoring oil combined with white chocolate tastes nearly exactly like the cookies, creating a super-sweet and extra-fun bright pink drink.

MAKES 6 REGULAR COCOA BOMBS

12 ounces bright pink candy melts *or* white chocolate, tempered and colored bright pink
¼–½ teaspoon frosted animal cookies flavoring oil, to taste
1 recipe batch white hot cocoa mix (page 41) *or* ½ cup store-bought mix
½ cup mini dehydrated marshmallows
Frosted animal circus cookies, plus extra for decorating
2 ounces white candy melts *or* white chocolate, tempered
Rainbow nonpareil sprinkles

Melt the chocolate and thoroughly stir in the flavoring oil to taste. Pour 1–2 tablespoons melted chocolate into each mold and use a brush or the back of a spoon to make sure the chocolate fills in all of the mold and up the edges. Refrigerate 5 minutes to set. If the edges are thin, carefully brush more chocolate around the edges and refrigerate for 5 more minutes. Carefully unmold. Set aside 6 of the shells for the tops. Melt the edges of 6 of the shells that will be the bottoms. Fill these cocoa bomb shells with: 1 tablespoon white hot cocoa mix, a handful of marshmallows, and a few cookies. Then melt the edges of the other halves of the cocoa bombs, one at a time, and stick them to the bottom halves. Let set. Melt the 2 ounces of candy melts or white chocolate, and add to a piping bag with a very fine tip or a plastic bag and snip the corner to create a very small opening. Pipe lines across the tops of the finished cocoa bombs. Decorate with rainbow nonpareil sprinkles.

To Make: Place a hot cocoa bomb in the bottom of a mug. Add 8–10 ounces of very hot milk and stir well. Microwave for 10–20 extra seconds and stir well again for best taste. Adding whipped cream and more sprinkles might be too indulgent, but . . . when have I ever said no to whipped cream?

Resources

Chocolate
Guittard
Ghirardelli
Merckens
Wilton's

Cocoa Mixes
Four Brothers Chocolate
Vosges Haut Chocolat
Tavernier Chocolates
Williams-Sonoma

Flavor Oils
LorAnn
Nature's Flavors
Amoretti
One on One/Get Suckered Flavors
Bickford Flavors

Sprinkles/Decorations
Fancy Sprinkles
Bakell
Sprinkle Pop
BakeDeco
Confectionery House
Layer Cake Shoppe
River Road Sprinkles

Glitter/Shimmer/Luster/Coloring Powders
Fancy Sprinkles
Confectionery House
Bakell

Other Flavors/Ingredients
Nuts.com for mini chips, candies, and freeze-dried fruits
Freshly Preserved for freeze-dried fruits and candy
Etsy for fondant and marzipan decorations and more
The Vermont Country Store for unique candies and fudge
Five Below

Packaging/Tools
EggCartons.com
ClearBags

Contributors
Four Brothers Chocolates: www.fourbrothers chocolates.com
Superfresh Café and owner Jessica Jean Weston: www.superfreshcafe.com
Tavernier Chocolates: www.tavernierchocolates .com

For updated links and resources, visit my website at www.nataliewise.com.